THE CHRISTMAS LETTERS

SIMON HOGGART is the parliamentary sketch-writer and diarist for the *Guardian*. He also writes about wine and TV for the *Spectator* and is the former host of Radio 4's *News Quiz*. Atlantic Books published *Don't Tell Mum: Hair-Raising Messages Home from Gap-Year Travellers* in 2006. His collection of parliamentary sketches covering the Blair era, *The Hands of History*, was published in 2007.

The
Christmas Letters

THE ULTIMATE COLLECTION OF ROUND ROBIN LETTERS

Simon Hoggart

Atlantic Books
London

First published in two separate volumes as *The Cat that Could Open the Fridge* in 2004 and *The Hamster that Loved Puccini* in 2005 in Great Britain by Atlantic Books, an imprint of Grove Atlantic Ltd.

The Cat that Could Open the Fridge © Simon Hoggart 2004
The Hamster that Loved Puccini © Simon Hoggart 2005

This paperback edition, with a new introduction by Simon Hoggart, published in 2007 in Great Britain by Atlantic Books.

Introduction © Simon Hoggart 2007

ISBN 978 1 84354 667 2

A CIP catalogue record for this book is available from the British Library.

3 5 7 9 8 6 4 2

Printed in Great Britain by
Clays Ltd, St Ives plc
Text design by Lindsay Nash

Atlantic Books
An imprint of Grove Atlantic Ltd
Ormond House
26–27 Boswell Street
London
WC1N 3JZ

Contents

Introduction

DEAR ALL,

Well, what a busy year it's been! Where to start? The main job, apart from looking after our amazingly talented children, enjoying luxury holidays in some of the world's most exotic places – or crossing them on a very grumpy camel [!] – building a new conservatory, organizing our local opera festival (though I say it myself, to rather gratifying acclaim!) and being frequently promoted at work, has been producing the book you hold in your hands!!!!

To be frank, and to lapse into non-newsletter English, it hasn't been that much work, since this consists of two books that have been published separately as hardbacks, *The Cat that Could Open the Fridge* and *The Hamster that Loved Puccini*. *Cat* was published in 2004, and *Hamster* the following year. They clearly touched a nerve. There can hardly be a family in the land that hasn't received one of these letters, and there can hardly be a reader who at some time hasn't uttered a cry of rage and despair before flinging them into the waste basket or recycling bin. The worst thing about any affliction is having to bear it alone, and I suspect the books had the remedial effect for many people of demonstrating that others were suffering too. Just knowing that can help relieve the pain.

I first started receiving round robin letters, or Christmas newsletters as some drearily persistent pedants insist they should be called, about ten years ago. (The modern usage of 'round robin', originally a shipboard petition, certainly dates back to the 1940s.) One phenomenon I've noticed is that some people hate them so much that it's often not enough just to throw them away; they need to get them out of the house, which seems to be a form of exorcism. Some people even find that ripping them up is not an adequate response; they tape them back together before sending the results on. If the senders recognize themselves in the *Guardian*, for which I write a column, or inside the covers of this book, they think, so much the better. They deserve to be punished. Indeed, some readers demand that I name and shame the writers, though I think this would be unfair. They may be smug, boastful and self-regarding, or in some cases unhappy souls who want to inflict all their sorrows upon others – presumably on the principle that if a trouble shared is a trouble halved, then one wished upon 100 people is reduced in effect to 1 per cent. But they deserve their privacy. For that reason, all the names in these two books have been changed, though I have tried to reflect age and class. So a Tarquin in the original letter might become a Tristan but not a Wayne; Edith could be Doris, but not Sharon.

The first letters came to me at the *Guardian*, from readers who hoped I might describe the terrible effect they can have on some recipients. Sometimes this was possible, but not easy, given the constraints of a newspaper column. Frequently the effect of the letters is cumulative: academic success for the children is followed by a highly paid new job for the father, a wonderful trip somewhere expensive, and glad tidings about a new vacuum cleaner. Almost as often the reverse is true: difficulties at work are matched by troubles with teenagers, a camping holiday in France when it rains six days out of seven, and ongoing problems with the septic tank. Indeed, the title of *The Cat that Could Open the Fridge* comes from a 2,000-word letter in which the writer suffers almost every misfortune modern man can undergo – mostly medical, but including a broken-down car, a ride on the London Eye in mist and rain, and various mishaps befalling his children. Then at the end, he reveals that the family's pet cat has learned how to open the fridge, so leading to every pet-owner's nightmare: the animal that can help itself.

Some readers and friends thought a collection of the letters would work, but I was doubtful. Reprinting them in full would be as tedious an experience for people who bought the book as it had been for the original recipients. Yet many required lengthy contemplation to release the full horror, rather in the way that a fine wine needs time and space to breathe before it reveals its qualities. It was Jane Turnbull, now my agent, who spotted that a mixture of brevity and wordiness might work. I am very grateful to her for her ideas and encouragement, and to Toby Mundy, the head of Atlantic Books, for his encouragement, and money.

As I said, the book touched a nerve, and material continued to pour in. The result was a new book, *The Hamster that Loved Puccini*. The title came from a letter in which it was reported that a family pet who nibbled indifferently on its food while other operatic composers were on the CD-player, would leap on to his wheel and start spinning joyfully the moment 'One Fine Day' or 'Your Tiny Hand is Frozen' began. This was clearly a joke, or at least a coincidence, so the tale served to illustrate the way some round robin writers were becoming more self-aware, more ironic, anxious not to take themselves too seriously.

People often ask how these letters started. I'm not certain, but I'm pretty sure they began in the United States, where most social trends see the light of day. American families are often spread far and wide; folk will happily up sticks and move from Maine to New Mexico, Oregon to Florida, leaving behind family and close friends. The Christmas, or holiday newsletters, as they are generally known there, are perfect for filling in the gaps in people's lives. If the writers have lived next door for more than fourteen years, then you want to know how Gwen is getting on in college and whether Frank's new job worked out. A disproportionately large number come from the Commonwealth, and for the same reason. The tone varies from smug to slightly desperate: 'Look, we made the right decision. Yes, we miss Nan, but it's sunny almost every day, the kids spend every weekend at the beach, the wine is great...' Everything is compared to the old country and the letters seek to validate the writer's decision to abandon it.

When did they become so numerous? By a slow but steady growth, linked to the development of technology. (I like the fantasy of Mrs William Caxton writing the first ever round robin in 1477: 'I haven't seen much of Will lately – he's been far too busy playing with his new German "printing press". Boys and their toys, eh?'.) Centuries later, carbon paper in a typewriter would produce three readable copies, and two more which nobody could make out. The Gestetner or Roneo made it easy for people to make a 'stencil' which could then be rolled on to a drum and used to print as many copies as you wanted. But almost nobody had access to one of these at home. Then came the photocopier, which could be used at work, provided you didn't make it too obvious. This meant that almost anyone – almost anyone with a middle-class office job, that is – could print off as many copies as they wanted quickly and easily. (The newsletter is very middle class; I can't think of one I've read that clearly comes from a working-class family. That's not to say that all the writers are well off; many are members of the *nouveaux pauvres*, working in less well-paid white-collar jobs, such as librarians and teachers.)

But of course it was the home computer that made mass pro-duction of newsletters both easy and satisfying. For the first time pictures could be reproduced properly ('Jill in party mode! Pssst! Don't anybody let on it was the big Five-0!'; 'Harry, proud captain of the team which won the regional cup for under-11's.')

Decorations appeared in the margins, their jollity sometimes in inverse proportion to the content of the letter, so that news of a painful hernia operation might be accompanied by laughing Santas and sprigs of holly. The home computer now means that you can run off endless letters at a keystroke: when the machine asks 'Number of copies?' you type in '100', and go off to make a cup of tea. As it happens, almost nobody has 100 friends (or at least 100 people who want to know every detail of your lives, which is a different thing). That's why so many wind up in the hands of people who really don't want them. 'I knew these people when they lived next door to my brother, 15 years ago. I have no interest in them or their lives or their four wonderful children...' 'I met this man at a conference in Derby when we had a couple of drinks together. Big mistake! It has condemned me to receiving this annual farrago of boastful nonsense.'

Self-publishing has been booming since computers made it so cheap. I have been sent one American letter in the form of a 200-page book. Some recipients take revenge. One family is so incensed by an arrogant round robin they get every year that they scrawl offensive remarks about the letter all over it. Then the next one to visit another city posts it back from there, so that the senders can never work out which of their unlucky readers is doing it. I feel slightly hurt on behalf of these people, although there is a simple remedy: stop sending the things.

Some people imagine it's an age thing and that most of the

letters come from the elderly and retired. That is not the case. The impulse to start sending often seems to come with setting up a first home. Some children start to help 'write' the family letter from birth, and in one terrible example here, while still *in utero*.

Again, people sometimes wonder which letters are most enraging. I'm afraid that, like all journalists, I often find that what is most annoying or disastrous makes the best material. It's like the probably true tale of the hack in Northern Ireland who sees a massive bomb explosion and says, 'Wow, great story!' In the same way the more conceited or dementedly over the top a letter is, the more I relish it, even if it has made the original recipient gibber with rage. I suspect, though, that the worst of all are those from the proselytizing religious, most especially those who see God's hand in all the good things that happen to them, and blithely ignore the pain and misery suffered by others. The implication that, if you share their faith, you too will have beautiful, clever children and take your holidays in the Maldives, is enough to drive anyone to homicide.

As the media pressure continues, a degree of self-awareness is creeping in. But the sheer quantity of letters seems to be as great as ever – if not greater, since more people are learning how to make use of their home computers. Every year I appeal for *Guardian* readers to send in their choicest examples, and every year several hundred arrive. Here are some recent – and like every other letter in this book, entirely genuine – examples that came in after the first volumes were originally published. Children still have the starring roles in most missives: 'Not only does Tami know how to spell words such as "bisect" and "exhaust" (year 4 key spelling skills) but she also knows many of her multiplication tables.' We are not told how old Tami is – she might be seventeen, for example.

Sometimes parents hint at disappointments: 'Harry has got a job working in a KFC in the motorway service station' does not imply that the glittering prizes are in view. Or, of a teenager, 'she is growing in confidence and can now take buses on her own.' Some sad medical history there, perhaps. 'Rowan has a part-time job working in a chic restaurant and gets to meet some of Newcastle's A-list celebrities.' I wonder who's on the B-list?

Recipients remain just as cross. 'I have met this woman twice in my life, and have never set eyes on any of the innumerable people mentioned in her wretched letter,' is typical. An English couple living in Chicago list no fewer than 108 names in their letter. They lead a dizzying life amid the arts: 'The year really began when we celebrated Mozart's birthday.' Another letter, from Yorkshire, mentions well over 100 people, including seventeen new ones in a nine-line passage. None at all are introduced or identified. 'This is from a boyhood friend of my husband who we have seen perhaps twice in 40 years!' protests one reader. The letter to this almost complete stranger includes details of an unpleasant operation: 'a new procedure which entails shortening the bowel by cutting out a short section and stapling the two ends together'. Well, if you hit 'Print 100' lots of people have to be told.

Humour makes welcome appearances more often now. This chap's wife goes with some friends on holiday to Morocco, 'where a cocky young Arab offered 10,000 camels for her. Nothing like enough, but what would I do with *more* than 10,000 camels?'

On the other hand, senders still confuse whimsy with humour, and many continue to write as if from their pet. This is from Parker, a cat living in Lancashire: 'Rite now i is sitting on Mary's lap on the computer, diktating a nise letta to you all. I do not always like it when Mary is on the computer becoz i is not the centre of attention…' The whole letter is spelled in similar style. Do they imagine anyone will finish it?

Another reader gets a letter every year in which the boasting drives him into something like a cardiac-inducing fury. 'I once accidentally tuned into *Gardeners' Question Time* and there was the writer herself. "I have an enormous garden of 23 acres. Could the panel advise?"'

Others feel unable to skate over the fact that their lives may not be packed with excitement. 'I am head of information systems, and the team bought me a nice cake for my 49th birthday.' A couple living in the Midlands pay a visit to Tewkesbury, 'where we visited a fascinating carpet shop'. In October, they joined neighbours for a trip to Wales. 'We were just one hour from home when the bus broke down. We were only one hour late, so it could have been worse.' Small pleasures lodge in some people's minds – some very small. 'In April we went to Finsbury Park and looked at grandmother's old house.'

Misery remains a favourite theme: 'Jim started the year badly with appendicitis, then Stuart's arm was in plaster when he missed the landing mat during the high jump. Terry ended up with an infected elbow and Olly started treatment on a rugby injury (still not sorted). After the summer holidays, Stu broke his leg (rugby). Within five days Mum had a heart attack (better now), my sister needed her head stitching, Olly was stung by a jellyfish, and our dog needed an emergency op.'

But that is all jolly fun compared to the 'irksome and sad events' suffered by another family. The wife, whose hobby is ballroom dancing, is nearly made redundant, and her new job at the firm is not as satisfying as the old one. She and her husband go on a cruise, but it is cold and it rains every day. Their car is written off in an accident, one friend commits suicide and another dies of a heart attack. They get stuck on the M4 and so miss her funeral. And to top it all, 'I have become a martyr to my knees. It rather spoils the picture when I twirl in my frothy dress and expose two thick elasticated knee supports.'

Exotic holidays and homes abroad still play a big part in the letters. This family from north-eastern England went to Mongolia, where 'we drank fermented mare's milk, ate roast marmot, and experienced the humbling hospitality of those who have nothing but share everything. Other highlights included a Buddhist temple and meeting Brian Blessed.' Eh?

And, of course, some regard their round robin as a direct mail shot. One couple from Devon bought a flat by the sea in Montenegro, and enclose the brochure, which records, 'as a friend, you will receive a 10% discount (5% extra in second week)'. Thanks!

A final word on how the book is organized. *Cat* is divided roughly into subject matter, with a quote from a particularly choice letter as the title of each chapter. So, the little diamond is yet another dazzlingly successful child, the pyramids (overrated) head the travel section, and of course the cat that could open the fridge is about all the misery that humanity is heir to.

Hamster was organized in a slightly different way. I noticed how the same unforgivable traits afflict round-robiners, so it seemed sensible to group the letters into seven categories of various 'sins', such as mawkishness, whimsy, sanctimony and smug self-satisfaction. Some, of course, are guilty of all seven.

I do find all these letters fascinating, even those which don't provide a usable quotation. For a nosy parker like me, it's a little like walking down a residential street in autumn, a time when curtains are still open but lights go on in front rooms, providing a brief tableau (it's important not to stare in) of other people's lives: a family watching TV, a row, a young couple together, or an elderly couple dancing to an unseen gramophone. I hope you enjoy these glimpses into the lives of others as much as I do.

The Cat that Could Open the Fridge
——

A Little Diamond to Polish

IF THERE IS one thing that is absolutely guaranteed to enrage the recipients of round robin letters, it is news of other people's wonderful children. Why do these paragons never seem to fail their exams, throw teenage tantrums, or hang out with unsuitable friends? Why do they spend so much time on their schoolwork and their musical instruments (including, in some cases, 'flugelhorns', heaven help us), and why do they never spend time slumped in front of *Neighbours*, or a computer game? How is it they always get to their first choice university, and never have to settle for a former polytechnic because they got two Cs and a D? Surely some of them do drugs, or at least go binge-drinking? Why do they seem so much better, so much more unutterably perfect, than our own children?

Not all of them, of course, and a very few round robins include brats and teenage nightmares. But it would be hard to keep the contents of such a letter from the eyes of the children themselves, and so many writers think too much honesty might be unwise. Instead, natural parental pride and the desire of middle-class families to encourage their offspring means that we, the readers, are furnished with almost exclusively happy news. It is most people's experience of teenagers that they must be even more embarrassed by the buckets of praise tossed over them than they would be by criticism. What seventeen-year-old would risk another seventeen-year-old reading about their devotion to academic work or, come to that, the Grade V in a musical instrument played by only seven other people in the entire world?

> JACQUELINE *our eldest daughter will be ten in February. She is kind and gentle and cares for anyone who is sad... she has wonderful perception. Her sister Luciana is eight. She is a live wire — wants to be doing something every minute of every day. Art and craft are her particular passions. She has thick blonde hair with big blue eyes. She has plenty of personality and at the end of a rough or a long day her energizing hugs are the best medicine I have ever known.*

> IN MARCH, *Kati gained distinction for Grade IV theory and is currently awaiting the result of Grade V flugelhorn.*

> LEXIE *settled into school from Day One, has made crowds of friends, and is more than surviving. Academically, I caught her reading her Latin textbook the first weekend, as she wanted to know more about it... her grades have been brilliant. Poppy has just been a King in the school nativity play, which was the most brilliant nativity play I have ever seen.*

Other people are pressed in to line up and join the chorus of parental praise.

HARVEY *was nine on August 1st, and commands serious respect at a daunting 5'2". His teachers at his primary school have nothing but praise both for his achievements and his character. He completed his Amateur Swimming Association level 12 this summer... he began trombone lessons in September and already plays in the school band. In the Christmas performance, based on themes in the 1960s, he took on the role of Bobby Moore and was an enthusiastic participant in the Sheffield peace march.*

TIM *has made a big impression at his new school, especially on the headmaster, who keeps having him in his study for a chinwag.*

That was written without evident irony, which may say something about either Tim's behaviour or the headmaster's proclivities. Of course being the Leonardo of your day doesn't necessarily mean you walk into the finest summer jobs.

JESSICA *got her A-levels (straight As) despite going to every party in NW London for the whole year, and has therefore got into her university of first choice, Bristol, to read Drama in 2004 — there were only two deferred places and over one thousand applicants! She even got a mention in the school newsletter! Broadway, here we come! First, she is working in W H Smith's.*

No child in these letters ever has to be dragged unwillingly to piano practice, or forced to pick up a detested musical instrument.

WHERE to start? Let's start with little Titus who is turning into a very competent violin player. He is set for his first public performance at church over Christmas, and pleased as punch to be playing with the big ones. Terri's church music group goes from strength to strength; Ariadne and Jolyon play regularly. Jolyon has a music scholarship from the education department and if we tell you that he has a special solo playing Lisa's sax part in the Simpsons theme you'll get a feel for how much he loves to play. It seems that when he picks up his sax it's just an extension of his body. Where does Jolyon end and the music begin?

SOPHIE is a creature of habit, gaining a Merit in every music exam she's ever taken. This year was no exception, with Merits of Grade 5 piano and flute. She also took her first dancing exam in July with Grade 3 Tap, for which she was awarded... yes, a Merit, with 8 1 per cent. This was something of a surprise to us, as the sentence 'an elephant is a graceful bird' has always sprung to mind with her.

HARD to believe that Tasha will be ten on the 9th! She still enjoys swimming, and will go and do thirty lengths. She plays both the piano and the clarinet, so the words 'have you practised your piano and clarinet?' are often heard in our house.

ALISON has had a very musical year playing her trumpet in various bands and orchestras. She went off to Prague with a school music trip and has recently played in the Royal Festival Hall with our county schools symphony orchestra. She continues with her *piano, ballet and Duke of Edinburgh award scheme, even though this is her GCSE year.*

FELICITY *is a passionate, compassionate eleven-year-old. She loves maths and sciences along with the arts and technology. She enjoys being a wandering minstrel, walking round the house, playing her violin.*

But it's never enough for these kids to be good at just one, or even three things.

MARTIN *sings so well he was made Head Chorister at school, and will be introducing the chamber choir at the concert hall in December. He is still learning the piano and flute. He still loves sport too and was delighted to hear the sports and music teachers fight over him to be Sports Captain rather than Head Chorister.*

AMBER *is now in full time school; she loves her school and literally runs to her classroom every morning. Early in the year she was awarded a merit badge for her class, and she has been chosen to play Mary in the upcoming nativity play. She will have the opportunity to sing a solo. Outside school she takes dance, music and swimming lessons and in her down time she always has a marker, crayon or paint brush in her hand. Our Christmas cards this year were entirely designed by Amber.*

All that from a five-year-old. But there is no end to the talents of our writers' children.

HARRY *was 'Jesus' in the school 'Jesus Christ, Superstar'.*
This was the best production I have ever seen, youth or adult.
The organization is wonderful and all the children gain so much.
Both boys, especially Harry, were physically and emotionally
drained at the end of it. I was drained too — seeing your son
crucified nightly is not an experience I would recommend —
especially when he calls out for his mother!

When they tackle sport, these children naturally make it almost to the top.

GREG *has also been chosen for the school rugby team, partly we*
believe because he has no fear.

Some readers have sent me whole series of letters from successive years. This has enabled me, for example, to keep up with Amy's astonishing success in her girls' cricket team, with detailed descriptions, season by season, of how many runs she scored and how many wickets she took. Girls in particular are now into boys' sports.

CASSANDRA *made a great start in secondary school this year.*
Better than we could have hoped for. Her number one sport
continues to be soccer. She also signed up for water polo, which
necessitated being at the pool 7 a.m. on Monday mornings. (I was
thrilled, being the morning person I am. Ha ha!) She joined the
school concert band and jazz band. Having played the alto sax for

*ten years, she was also asked to play the tenor sax, so she heads off
to band practice with a sax in each hand. She has made a lot of
friends and is popular in her year… she again played soccer in two
teams through the winter, with the boys' team on Saturdays and
girls on Sundays. One of the boys paid her the ultimate compliment
when he told his Dad 'we'll be in trouble today as Cassie won't be
playing.'*

JACQUI *manages to train as a surgeon while fitting in diving trips
to Thailand, Cayman, Cuba and the Red Sea. We've told you about
Tori's sporting prowess, and at number 5 in the world, she is not
doing badly!*

THE BOYS *have a heavy training schedule. They also have a
hamster.*

The recipient wrote in the margin of that letter: 'no doubt soon
to be entered in the World Hamster Wheel speed championships.'
Of course these happy children do have a lot of help from their
supportive, or perhaps at times oppressive, parents.

NATASHA *continues at our local university in political science. She
is devouring history and politics and this year took on Spanish, as
she is planning a trip to Latin America next summer. To give her a
helping hand, I hired a cleaning lady from El Salvador, so she can
have some conversation practice.*

Possibly learning how to shout, 'and why is my bed not made at 4 in the afternoon?' in faultless Spanish.

Not only do these children have a tremendous cultural and intellectual life, but their diet is pretty near perfect too. No worries about childhood obesity among these dietary paragons:

SHE IS *incredibly fit and lean, eats virtually no sweets, loves Granny Smith apples, and drinks loads of fruit juice.*

WE MUST *have one of the most varied and healthy diets of anyone in the country — though chilli, coriander and ginger do tend to turn up rather more often than potatoes. Jack and Lulu would like to be reminded what a chip is!*

Oh, I don't know. I suspect the occasional sneak visit to McDonald's for Jack and Lulu, on the way home from school.

Sometimes there's just so much going on, it's hard to cram it all into one letter:

IN MARCH, *Stephanie passed her Grade 5 ballet exam with flying colours and Richard appeared in a concert with the newly named* Compagnie des Chansons... *we were in the village production of* As You Like It. *I played Phoebe (a heartless shepherdess) and Stephanie sang beautifully... in July Stephanie passed her Grade 4 piano exam, with merit, and Peter spent his last few days at primary school. He rounded off the summer term with a snarlingly wonderful performance as the Sheriff of Nottingham. He had great fun in his solo, pushing over schoolmates and stealing flowers from little girls… in November, Peter appeared in another wonderful* Chansons *concert. Stephanie has just taken her saxophone Grade 5 — we await the results.*

And we know exactly what those results will be, without having to wait, with bated breath, for next year's letter.

It is certainly true that if the children of people who send round robins were any kind of guide, there would be no problems at all in our educational system.

WE HAD *a fleeting but memorable breakfast at Heathrow as Isobel flew out and Holly flew in. Memorable because we had with us, unopened by order, Holly's GCSE results, 5 As and 5 A*s. Celebrating at Heathrow is not our usual style, but we managed it pretty well!… Holly's summer was one of contrasts. France and Spain with Dickon (Purdue) on a shoestring, in the course of which she acquired and hauled back 5lbs of volvic honey in her rucksack. This was followed by a fortnight languishing on expensive yachts in the Aegean with other beautiful women and apparently rather engaging young men. She was impressed by three things: the earthquake (6.7 on the Richter scale), which she was at the centre of; the lifestyle, which she found agreeable, and the fact that she knew more poetry than the Poet Laureate's son, who was one of the engaging young men.*

Many layers of tooth-furring smugness are slotted in there! The letter even includes footnotes, in this case a reminder of the hilarious time that someone in the family brought back fifteen gallons of Greek olive oil – as hand baggage!

Sometimes things do go just a little wrong. Nobody wants horrid things to happen to children, though it can be hard to stifle a smirk:

> JACK *is continuing with his bagpipe playing and at the moment the house is very quiet, as he is away training and racing in Italy and Austria. His skiing is coming on well and the highlight was being chosen for the regional ski team. He skied in the International Cup in Turkey where he managed to get an individual bronze medal and was part of the team which won the gold medal for the first time. He also managed to be in a lift which was overcrowded and crashed down a number of floors in Istanbul, but that is another story.*

Schools exist primarily to reflect parents' views of their own children.

> AMELIA *continues to learn how to play the trumpet, has taken up drama, represents the school in a host of sports, and even copes with cross country running without too many murmurs of disapproval. At a recent parents' evening, it was good to hear how well she is thought of by all her teachers.*

This is from a British family living in the US.

> ELEANOR *is a 'straight A' student, excelling in maths and science,*
> *but also a truly good all-rounder. She is playing clarinet and was*
> *recently accepted by our local youth symphony orchestra. This was*
> *an amazing achievement as she is the only twelve-year-old in the*
> *orchestra and the youngest by three years... Melanie is also doing*
> *incredibly well. She was recently tested and although she's still just*
> *eight, was shown to have a reading age of twelve. At a recent*
> *parent / teacher meeting I asked the teacher if there were any areas*
> *of weakness with Melanie that we should be working on, and her*
> *reply was 'no, you've given me a little diamond, and all I have to*
> *do is polish it.'*

You might imagine that the return to the UK after time in America
might be difficult. Not for our writers' offspring!

> LEO *and Cassie had a busy year, which started with sitting exams*
> *for UK schools (groan!). They continued to play American Youth*
> *soccer (football), both reaching their respective finals. Their karate*
> *has improved tremendously, standards in the UK being much more*
> *exacting than in the US... Leo has continued with guitar lessons*
> *and Cassie is in a local drama programme. They got excellent*
> *reports from their school in Philadelphia, and have made a great*
> *return to school life in the UK. Way to go, Leo and Cassie!*

Such wonderful offspring keep at it. They don't let leaving school, their first great arena of achievement, slow them down one bit.

> ELIZABETH *is in her final year at Oxford and is president of her*
> *college law society. She hosted the annual dinner, with Cherie*
> *Booth as guest of honour. Ms Booth was extremely charming, but*
> *gave an earnest and boring half-hour speech. So Elizabeth had an*
> *easy job bringing the evening back to life, and managed to make*
> *the honoured guest squirm, on three occasions. Lizzie also spent the*
> *summer in Vietnam, Cambodia and Thailand.*

Of course you know that this account must have come from Elizabeth, the latter-day Cicero, herself. I wonder if Cherie Blair got a thank-you note for her time and trouble.

If nearly all children are perfect, grandchildren can attain almost celestial levels of beauty, grace, skill and adorability. Round robinners love their exclamation marks, or as journalists call them, 'screamers'. Some letters resemble the shower scene in *Psycho*:

> PATSY *is now fine, and in all our eyes the cutest, cleverest, and most*
> *advanced baby in the world!!!!!!!! Just recently she made her first*
> *trip to Burnley, flying up with her Mum and Aunty, loving every*
> *minute of the long wait in the airport!!*

> PATRICK *is nearly as tall as I am (which is not difficult!!) and*
> *Pam was overwhelmed with the praise she received about him at*

parents' night. Is there anything he doesn't do well for his age?
The answer is no.

SHE IS *a complete joy and apart from the first 6 weeks when she*
hardly seemed to sleep has been an angel-child ever since, full of
smiles and giggles, rarely crying, sleeping through the night, eating
anything and everything that we offer her. What have we done to be
so blessed??!!

Sold your souls to Beelzebub, most parents would guess. Actually
this letter radiates considerable smugness, the writer adding on
the next page:

CAN IT *get any better than this? Living in a lovely house with 'my*
girls' in a great village community, with a pub which brews and
sells award-winning beer...

With some parents, a brief description of their offsprings' limitless
virtues can never be quite enough. This is about a newborn infant
('the most adorable personality we could ever have wished for').

FOR THOSE *of you who have access to the Internet, Josh has his*
own website, where you can view the latest pictures and video clips
of him. Just go to www... and follow the instructions. Email us if
you have any problems.

'Yes, your perfect child keeps appearing on my screen as a pop-
up!' possibly.

But all is not without flaw in our letter-writers' Eden. Sometimes children fail to come up to the high standards expected of them. This, however, can rarely be admitted, since, as we have noted, the disappointing children might read the letter. Writers have to skirt around the topic.

> HENRY *delighted us all by getting a first at Wadham. Tibby has gone the Cambridge route, and has just started to read Economics at The (!) Queen's College. Susie, well, she is our joy and our delight, bringing happiness and laughter into our lives.*

Oh dear, learning difficulties there, we suspect. Similar problems seem to have afflicted this family:

> THE CHILDREN *are all thriving. Jack is doing wonderfully well at prep school, India continues to excel at ballet, and Tara is riding, both passing exams and winning competitions with flying colours. Xanthe is eccentric and charming and keeps me smiling.* [uh oh] *Kinvara talks incessantly and is a guinea-a-minute!* [another euphemism, I fear] *There is never a dull moment, specially since I dispensed with the nanny in February!*

Or

> EUAN *is doing well at everything he attempts, swimming, football, martial arts, Beavers, and somehow fitting in schoolwork, to great effect. All that, and only six. Archie is the light in the darkness. A more contented, animated, and lovable child we have yet to find.*

Again, you wonder what we are not being told.

Here's another, making it plain which child has performed its duties to the parental satisfaction. Note how the writer has explained precisely how SATs work, so that everyone can appreciate fully the attainments of at least one daughter.

> HARRIET *is sailing through school — works hard and gets brilliant grades. I saw the entire year's results as they came to the junior school. She was one of four children, in a year of 250, to get two level sevens and one eight in her year 9 SATs (that is the highest possible these days). She was also the only one to get more than one level eight in her grades for the year, and she got five. For those of you who are 'out' of education, that is what you are expected to get when you take GCSEs, which is in two years' time. That is my boast for this year. She is also lovely, which is far more important (whoops, that is another boast!). She has written something which is being used for the Cathedral service I mentioned earlier. Luke is plodding, still struggling to overcome dyslexia and dyspraxia and Lauren plays schools when she is not at the real thing! Harriet is in the schools' symphony orchestra, and was selected by the county to try for the national orchestra...*

Don't you feel so very sorry for Luke and Lauren?

Often letters hint at something the writers do not wish to relive:

> ROSE *thankfully ditched her boyfriend, who was causing us so much trouble last year.*

> TAMSIN, *eighteen, is doing so, so well. She is nearly double the weight she was two years ago.*

With so much achievement, so many successes, the orchestras and sports stadia of Britain being filled with the children of our round robinners, it seems awfully unfair that for a minority — admittedly a tiny minority if these letters are anything to go by — things can go wrong.

> TOBY'S *life never seems to be straightforward. In addition to his pain — he is waiting for an operation to sever some of his nerves — he has suffered harassment from a previous girlfriend on the course which has, alas, severely affected his relationship with the other students and did not help him in dealing with his pain. He has no shortage of admirers, but is trying to be very choosy after his latest problems. He is looking forward to leaving Loughborough University — sadly he has recently had to resign from the special police force there.*

This, after lavish praise of several siblings:

> PORTIA *is a different matter. She is a hedonist, does not like hard work, and has an inflated idea of her own achievements.*

But at least she sounds nicer than her parents. Sometimes children can let you down in the most unexpected ways.

EARLY *in the summer, Emily's teacher told us that her nose was becoming disruptive and what were we doing about it? The poor child has always been terribly snotty; if you could sell it, we'd be millionaires by now... weeks of nose-drops have achieved nothing. This year's teacher hasn't complained, but I think she's slightly deaf.*

It is rare for these children not to reach the highest levels of attainment. But occasionally it does happen.

MEGAN *is no longer working in the burger van. She now lives with Charlie in Neasden – 'aiming high as usual' said Jenny at the time of the burger van, when she moved in with Charlie to his flat which is in a multi-storey car park (believe it or not!). However, they seem very happy and Megan says the flat is very nice from the front, though we've only seen it from the back, which you get to via the rather unpleasant service road, but turn off before the car park barriers at the entrance.*

This last extract is remarkable as the fiercest attack on a writer's child that I have ever found in any of the hundreds of letters which recipients have sent in. But it is also rather magnificent. The last paragraph is, I think, a tribute to the resilience, stamina and sheer bloody optimism of all round robinners:

THE CONCLUSION *of this year's story is mixed. We may, sadly, have seen the end of Chloe, having been persuaded to help her with* short-term loans and a deposit to get her new flat. In return she has broken every promise on the repayments and given us such unbelievable verbal abuse that we really want nothing more to do with her. She seems to have little to show for all the money she has obtained, so we hate to think of what we might have unwittingly financed. The good news is that we are determined to have a good finish to the year, so we are off the Dordogne for Christmas, testing a new caravan! We'll be thinking of you!

The Stubbed Toe Blackspot

TOO MUCH INFORMATION! That's the cry from so many of the people who shop the senders of circular letters. Take this one from a family in the Midlands. It is more than 6,000 words long, and includes almost an hour-by-hour description of their summer holiday.

FRIDAY 13TH: *(no bad luck so far!) Pick up euros, haircut, set off 11 a.m., made Dover by 2.20 with no stops, so in time for 2.30 crossing... watched survival and dating shows on French reality channel very similar to programmes at home... leisurely breakfast and back onto the A26 en* direction *Reims, Metz, Nancy. Stopped at mediocre* aire *– picnicking was not allowed, so ate sandwiches in the car...*

SUNDAY 15TH: *woken at 4.30 by birdsong, got up at 8.30, leisurely breakfast. Surprised not to have had a visit from the owners, but I said they would probably come at noon, which they did. We had asked to hire linen as our own wouldn't be the right size, but it was 11 p.m. before we had noticed, too late to bother them... the shopkeeper offered to hold our purchases while I fetched the car, to save Daphne struggling with a heavy box.*

There is disabled parking by the chemist opposite, but we didn't know
about it and parked in the all-day pay-and-display for 2 euros.

The holiday proceeded on its uneventful way. 'At 4.30 we hit the
village of Vinteilles, and discover – not a lot!' After supper they
take out a jigsaw:

UP AT 10.30, *more jigsaw – I did the bit Daphne doesn't like –*
I go through the whole box and sift all the sky into light, medium
and dark, sky with building, sky with foliage, sky with TV aerials;
then there are orange flowery bits, orange bricky bits and beigy bits.
I could have gone on but it was time to go out... [Friday] we spent
nearly all day on the jigsaw: with so many missing pieces and a
nightmarish amount of sky we reluctantly decided to give up at
22.30, and broke it up at 22.35.

But the fun doesn't end there. They go on to Le Touquet where
they sit on the beach...

WE CAME *to the (band) aid of a woman who had stubbed her toe,*
but the next person who stubbed his toe had friends with tissues.
It must have been a stubbed toe blackspot.

The puzzling thing is that if these people came round to your house
and described their trip in such detail you might wish to set the
dogs on them. But the people who write the letters seem unfazed.
Again, no detail of their holiday is too small, including this late
breakfast suffered by a Yorkshire family who went to Cornwall:

THE HOTEL *was largely staffed by surfers, who apparently dictated when they were prepared to work to the hotel owner. Dinner was late one night, possibly because the weather had tempted staff to stay out too long. We needed an early breakfast one morning, because of the need to arrive for the helicopter check-in at Penzance, and it was a very scratch meal, because the dining room did not open until fifteen minutes after the agreed time.*

This concerned an event that had happened fully three months previously. But there frequently seems to be an inverse proportion between the importance of the incident and the way it lodges in the minds of round robinners. This family holidayed in northern France.

WE HAD *coffee in the old fort, and I bought a stripy jersey, which led to me being taken for a Frenchman at a motorway service station checkout on the way home. While we were in Bronsac we had the excitement of a power cut during lunch. The staff had to add up 'l'addition' by hand!*

But it's not just holidays that come under the microscope. Even the absence of holidays can be described at wearisome length.

THE YEAR *started with snow (and a day without pay!) followed by not a lot until March, when it was visiting time. First, to Bletchley before Johnny and Trish went to Greece, then to Charles and Maggie at Andover. Easter came and went as a long weekend, at home doing gardening etc… for the rest of the summer I stayed local and gave foreign trips a miss this year. Not local was my annual trip to Scunthorpe to see Pru and Pete which coincided and included the Scunthorpe Beer Festival. Most of the beers were new, and made a change from Greene King.*

While some make a virtue of their dreary destinations:

JEREMY has travelled a number of times this year — but never to very exotic places, mainly Nottingham and Leicester. One trip to Leicester, he managed to stay over rather than travel the 160 miles home… amazingly, we have not gone to Center Parcs this year — somehow think we will have to plan a visit there next year, as we are well and truly CP fans.

I'll be chewing my fingernails waiting for next year's news! Home décor is also a popular topic:

AT THE END of May we took the bit between our teeth and started decorating the living room, as we are open plan, this also took us all the way up the stairs and included the upstairs hall. It took us 6 weeks!! Including 3 extra double power points, removing the previously filled Rawlplugs, endless rubbing down, lining, painting, the continuation of the laminate floor downstairs and equivalent flooring upstairs, yet more skirting and finding and laying carpet runners…

This work kept the same people away from their other love —

growing vegetables, and of course we need to be apprised of every shoot and tendril:

> DURING *our chaotic life our allotment did suffer this year. As usual we have had more than enough soft fruit and vegetables to keep us going over the next year as well as people avoiding us during the runner / French bean and courgette / marrow season. But we only came 39th in the borough's allotment competition, quite a drop from last year's 5th.*

Which leaves the question, why wait until the bean season to avoid these folk? You can steer clear of them every day of the week! On the other hand, they are not the only people to imagine that their plants are of limitless fascination to their acquaintance. Allotments do tend to dominate people's lives. This is one of only four paragraphs in a short letter from Wales:

> GROWING *your own fruit and veg can be very entertaining. The well-established crops, e.g. Jacqui's strawberries, did well, but the courgette experiment was doomed. The courgette seeds were planted but only one germinated. This courgette then turned out to be a cucumber! Next year we will buy courgette plants, rather than seeds.*

Those particular people are exceptional even by the standards of allotment lovers. No detail of their lives is too small to pass on to everyone else:

A GOOD JOURNEY *back to Cumbria was marred by the chronic bottleneck at the junction of the M5 / M6, but it is hard to find an easier alternative. Once back home we collected the cat, who had grown immensely during our holiday. Despite being absent from our house for six weeks, he settled in immediately, with none of the neurotic behaviour of his predecessor. He has grown into a very nice animal, very well-behaved, except in the vicinity of dried flowers.*

Curiously some people seem far more eager to provide you with masses of detail about what went wrong in their lives, and much less information about the good parts. This family in Scotland devote just over two lines to their Caribbean cruise, but nearly four times as much to their problems at the start:

MUST SAY, *the flight to London on BMI was one of the worst we could have been on, and could fill a chapter in a book. Suffice to say the flight was on a rolling half-hour late from 5 p.m., and took off at 7.30 p.m. for an hour flight. On arrival was stuck on the apron for 45 minutes because no parking space... locked in bus for another 45 minutes while driver found construction lorry driver who had parked at disembarkation point... not even an apology, although one steward did liven things up by calling an Italian lady stupid.*

There's a general rule that the people who tell you everything about their holiday will tell you everything about the rest of their lives. Take this family, who flew from Manchester to Majorca. They devote, quite literally, hundreds of words to the cost of parking and the shortcomings of the airport bar, adding on their return:

> THIS WAS FOLLOWED *by the clearing of the bungalow guttering and the painting of the fascia boards... another time an elderly friend fell in her flat, and we spent some time in the local casualty department! We decided to strip down an airing cupboard to the wood... the washing machine did not qualify for a new door seal, so had to be replaced... in October we had a bit of a 'do' with the neighbours... the video of parish footpaths is coming along – 49 out of 62 done so far. The memoirs are up to 1975 – lots of revelations, and hopefully some red faces if it ever gets into print!*

Heavens, if those revelations are up to the rest of this letter, publishers will be queueing around the block!

Most of us lead rather ordinary lives. What makes the writers of circular letters stand out is their belief that the ordinariness of their lives is fascinating to the rest of us. Take this, from the West Midlands:

> LIFE's *not all 'work'. We still go to the theatre regularly – even saw 'Cats' in Birmingham – excellent... We've been to quite a few outdoor shows this year such as the Shrewsbury Flower Show, Southport Flower Show and the Game Fair at Weston Park. I still swim twice a week. This is just a selection of our activities. No wonder I never seem to sit down. I'm exhausted just reading what we've done!!!*

This letter ends, rather sweetly:

> I HOPE *I haven't forgotten a vitally important item of news in my*
> *rush to get this done. With a bit of luck next year's epistle will*
> *report the culmination of the building work and decorating of our*
> *house and maybe even the garden. Watch this space!!!*

We will!!!

This next is part of a letter arranged chronologically, sent by a family in west London:

> FEBRUARY: *a peaceful month, punctuated by dental check-ups.*

Some use desktop publishing to produce mock newspapers. One from Scotland includes these headlines:

> NEW *paintwork in the shower room*
> *Jemima stars in school nativity play*
> *A summer of disappointing weather*
> *A visit to the Science Museum*

That final news story recalls that 'the high spot was the mouse found scurrying among the exhibits'.

Having builders in is exhausting and does tend to dominate people's lives. This is from the West Country:

> WE TOOK *the plunge and decided to extend our kitchen, which*
> *was something we had wanted to do ever since buying the house ten*
> *years ago. It had always been a daunting prospect as we knew that*

it could ruin the rather pretty back elevation of our house and that two flower beds would have to be destroyed... we decided to have the drive surfaced with tarmac. It was a problem to know what to do without breaking the bank. We hope that it will soon lose its blackness and turn more grey.

This from Lancashire:

THE GAS *men finally came on January 11. They were supposed to come at the beginning of December.*

Or this, from Hampshire:

DURING THIS *period and the ensuing months, we converted the cesspit into a septic tank.*

Elsewhere there are some exciting plumbing challenges:

THE COMPLICATION *on this occasion was blocked drains to the septic tank which, after hours of rodding, it was decided had to be replaced.*

A QUIET *family style Christmas for 2002? Yes, if you count the delights of installing a new toilet pan and plank-effect floor in our downstairs cloakroom!*

MY FRIEND *Ken came here in the spring and helped put up an attractive wooden roof (marine ply) on the 18ft garden shed — and after waterproofing it looks fine... also, without Ken's assistance, it would have been impossible to extend the landing over the stairs and to fit an extending drop-down ladder for easy access to the loft space. Now, after months fitting a loft floor…*

No, enough! But if you haven't had building work done yourself, you can always fill your readers in on what the offspring are up to:

JASON *and Penny are settled in Norwich and have been making some changes to their house. They now have a conservatory, which catches the sun during the day, and have changed some of their carpeted floors to wooden ones. Jason has insisted that everything that sits on the new floors must have felt feet.*

Occasionally people are so obsessed with building work that they even feel obliged to let the world know when there hasn't been any. This is the first paragraph in a 2002 letter from the south-east:

WE NEARLY *managed the year without working on the house, which was a relief. In October we did have to lay a floor in the utility, as the lino broke up.*

Meanwhile small domestic incidents are often ideal for filling in the otherwise empty pages.

I HAVE *a porch light, which has a sensor, which means that it's on when it's darkness. There is a lot of darkness over the year, which means that they don't last long. Come July 1 I went shopping for another. The first I bought flashed and flickered before it came on.*

I took it back to B&Q and said it does not work. They seemed surprised, but replaced it with another. That one did not work at all. By this time I was fed up and left it in the hall. For weeks I lived with a dark door, but then I found another at half the price.

This fascinating tale of domestic life was accompanied by a cartoon drawing of a light bulb, no doubt similar to the ones described in the dramatic narrative.

Here is just one incident from another letter, 3,000 words long:

OUR FIRST catastrophe of the year occurred whilst cleaning the oven; gravity lent a hand and the oven door fell to the floor. I was quite amazed at the distance broken glass can travel, and how it can shatter into such small pieces! ... The second catastrophe occurred when a lighted candle cracked its glass container and set fire to the top of the hi-fi/video unit... we now have a scorched top to the unit, but it could have been much worse.

Then, just as you think that a life so crowded with incident must have some moments of reflective calm:

WE HAD an unexpected trip to Bristol when Johnny locked himself out of the house! His next-door neighbour who has a spare key was not at home, so not wishing to disturb us, he waited for her to return. Then realizing his neighbour was away, felt it was too late to ring us and spent the night in his garage, finally ringing us the following morning!

Some round robinners' lives are so short of interesting material that they have to predict what they might get up to next year:

A VISIT *to the cinema is in the offing! Any ideas what to see?*

Others make you wonder how tedious a life can be for those who live it to record it and pass it on to others:

JAMIE *stayed and explored Peterborough, which has a Waitrose.*
He can't resist a good Waitrose.

While some are rather lacking in the irony department:

ROGER *has found the website of his old school, and now spends*
hours reading (and writing) about the Penfold Hall Old Boys.
I don't read it unless it's been left on my screen (Roger has his own
computer in the living room) and I fail to see the attraction. They
write trivial rubbish to each other and it is anything but uplifting.
A total waste of time, as Roger never knew 99.9 per cent of the
people who write, but it seems to keep him happy. Give me a good
book any day!

This attack on people who inflict the dreary detail of their lives on others is from a letter of nearly 3,000 words, which begins with a description of the different air fresheners in a B&B they stayed in on the south coast.

But then some people find their own day-to-day lives so fascinating they can't believe we don't want to share it with them.

This is part of an 850-word description of the writers' day. It's beautifully printed by computer with sprigs of holly around the edge, bringing a touch of seasonal magic:

> Do you *have routines? We do. Rise at 07.12 to the sound of Radio 3, down to the kitchen to make the tea, kettle having boiled on a time switch. Put in milk until the reflection of the light in the cups is covered. Take it up to the bedrooms, pour two cups. Turn on TV and watch* Breakfast *until the football comes on... Janet gets up, gets dressed and goes down for her breakfast and to make sure William gets his taxi to school. Used to be free, but now we have to pay a contribution. Meanwhile I shave with the super Philishave triple-head shaver Rod bought me for my birthday last year. Wonderful machine!... I weigh out 100 grams of mixed muesli and Grape Nuts with half a banana and eight grapes, orange juice and Aloe Vera, read* The Times, *starting with page 1... Thursdays Janet and I go to Sainsbury's, five miles away. I push the trolley and pick up things I fancy, choose the wine, while she does the real work, going down her list and sniffing out bargains. Shopping done, we have coffee and a bun, or biscuit.*

And so on and on until even the writer seems to realize that he may not be leading the most gripping life:

> Janet *read this and said, 'I think we are stuck in a rut!' I replied, 'well, it's a lovely rut!'*

Many fill their letters with photographs, usually reproduced very badly. Some, incredibly, give technical details: 'Even using ASA 400 film, I needed fill-in flash, as the afternoon had become cloudy'. Some are the kind of pictures you would throw in the bin as soon as you got them back from Boots. 'This is us, seen buying sausages at the butcher's shop.'

Other folk are just anally retentive. Take this couple in Australia, who use the cheap Virgin Blue airline to fly them around the continent. They spend almost as long describing the flights as on what they do when they get to where they're going.

> FOR *such air travel we have perfected the art of the in-flight meal. Virgin does not offer 'free' food or drink. On the other hand it allows people to bring their own food. To eat well without littering the cabin, we take: individual portions of a quality brie or camembert; some cherry tomatoes, a box of Carr's water biscuits (which are small enough to pop in the mouth — no crumbs), and for dessert, some fruit. A beer purchased on board helps to complement the cheese.*

It really does make one yearn to be knocking back champagne and lobster in first class, if only to sneer at their bite-size water biscuits.

Hobbies intrigue the hobbyist, though not necessarily his or her acquaintances:

> THE BEADERS *group met regularly at my house (average, seven of us) and we explored new techniques, the latest was for Christmas*

decorations. Here there was a breakthrough when we found we
could use clear floor polish for stiffening.

This next extract comes from a closely typed letter of around 9,000 words. It includes the sentence: 'We have accomplished many visits locally, and supported much of the local entertainment our town has to offer.' It also includes this:

THERE IS *now quite a business in trading railway ephemera – some*
steam locomotive plates are fetching five figures. I was pleased to
acquire a working timetable (that is, passengers and freight) for the
now extinct line from Abergavenny to Merthyr and its branches for
October 1912 when it was really busy. Some of the supplementary
information is quite fascinating, such as the official procedure for
cleaning horse boxes.

Some people feel obliged to record every social event they have attended. This is from the south-east:

As CHRIS *said, we had a brilliant summer and mine actually*
started in March / April – the weekly meeting with my Tuffaware
supervisor started off with coffee at home, progressed to a beer on
our patio, and ended up as two hours in the local pub garden.

The same writer proves that the spirit of Mr Pooter lives on:

A FRIEND *of ours has a brother, Les, and sister, Janet, who recently*
came out as gay. After a few beers (I still don't like wine) at a

dinner party, I said, 'I bet you never thought you'd have a brother and sister who were both Leses!' I think I got away with it, we're still speaking.

Others feel free to record even their most dreadful jokes.

BERTIE'S *middle daughter, Wendy, is married to a Scot of Italian extraction, and they have called their first child Guyano. Bertie asked, in his usual fashion, 'isn't that the posh name for seagull crap?' Fortunately it wasn't in the hearing of the proud Mum and Dad.*

So why tell us now?

Another letter from the Midlands contrived to bore the recipients with news of the Queen, which may take some doing.

I COULDN'T *bear to miss out when the Queen came to our cathedral to present the Maundy money purses to deserving citizens. So dressed 'to the nines' in best multi-coloured blouse & hat & royal blue jacket & skirt I got a ringside place in the Close, chatting to regular 'royal followers' from Liverpool about the cathedral's history while we all waited. I was watching Prince Philip, when suddenly THE QUEEN was right in front of us! 'Good morning, your Majesty,' said my companion. 'You've come a long way,' she said. 'Yes, Ma'am, but this lady lives and works here.' 'Oh?' said the Queen, turning to me. 'Yes, Ma'am,' says I, 'I'm a volunteer chaplain, here to talk to visitors.' 'Very good, well done!' and giving me the most beautiful smile, she moved on. As I said to James afterwards... not much, you might think... but when the Queen of England gives you her undivided attention, even briefly, IT'S A MIND BLOWING EXPERIENCE.*

For the Queen too, I'll wager. I hope she received a copy of the letter.

Jobs can be awfully dull, but that never inhibits our correspondents from telling us all about them. Imagine the teatime conversation in this home counties household:

JOHN has consolidated his knowledge of the intricacies of surveying equipment during the year and is still very happy. He succeeded in upgrading the ISO 9001 quality system in March, having beavered away writing three new manuals. The new BSI certificate on the wall makes it all seem worthwhile! Thelma has finally changed her company and she now works for a supplier of tills, or cash registers as you may know them.

This letter is from East Anglia:

I AM no longer group marketing manager for Astomia but am Business2Business manager at their light commercial vehicles site on the Diss Road (and in fact my director says he is really pleased about how the site is progressing and in how well we are doing! Now that is a first!) I really loved my job in marketing but felt it was time to move on and all the jobs I wanted to do had a certain element of Sales in them so I thought I would get a bit of sales experience. I also use quite a lot of my marketing techniques at the 4x4 and van centre, and I do enjoy a challenge. Unfortunately the hours of work seem to be longer — the pay is a little better but not as much as I would like. Ah well never mind. So if any of you want a van or a 4x4 I'm your man or woman.

A surprising element of confusion at the very end there...

Here's another fine example of the curious priorities observed by many round robinners. This letter is nine pages long, but devotes only two lines about the birth of a new granddaughter. However, there is an entire paragraph on the topic of a vacuum cleaner that broke down at an inconvenient moment. It ends like this, on a note that manages to be wonderfully perky and upbeat while simultaneously making the reader want to weep with boredom:

> WHEN *we retired the advice was to keep active, and so we have — just like being back at work! Now we have our Unitary Development Plan — Amendments and the Transport Board's Regional Public Transport Strategy requiring urgent study before meetings later this week. Finally, may we wish you all joy at Christmas and every happiness in the New Year.*

Computers are also a favourite topic. People who love these machines really love them. These folk actually built their own:

WE WERE *determined that it would be our last and no further upgrades ever!! For you technically minded, 'the beast' is a 350mhz Pentium II with 128 mg ram, 8.4 hard drive with an LS 120 mg floppy drive (5 times faster than the 1.4 floppies), Asus motherboard 100mhz bus, 40-speed CD-ROM, 8mg Matrox graphics card and a Soundblaster Gold AWE sound card...*

Please, haven't you got some news about your plumbing instead? Here's another computer nerd:

I WROTE *last time of replacing my PC, which was a seven-year-old case with four-year-old works. Those who know my methods will realize the many hours put into developing specifications and checking reviews. The Evesham Axis with AMD 2600 chip won the business... I bought a CRT rather than a flat screen. I am very pleased with it, but for some months it did have problems starting up, until they were diagnosed as a faulty motherboard which Evesham replaced at no cost. After nearly a year I have used 10 gigabytes and have just 65 left!*

The preparation of these letters can be a story in itself. One writer records a gripping incident from the previous year:

LAST *December I was late with this letter... I forgot to take my licking machine to London, so had to lick 80 stamps and envelopes myself, and the glue tasted so awful I had to keep making myself cups of hot Ribena.*

Sometimes people in supposedly glamorous jobs also have a dull time of it. Here's a tragic letter from an actor, sent to me by a famous actress, whom I won't name, because she really wishes the chap well:

> HAVING *finished playing WisheeWashee in Aladdin at the Pinetree theatre, I had a couple of months to myself* [a euphemism for the already euphemistic 'resting'] *before landing two jobs in one week. It started with a Burger King commercial in which I played an Easter Bunny and was followed by a corporate video for DH Evans. Within a few weeks of those, I was asked to take on two roles in Agatha Christie's* Ten Little Indians *at the Grand Theatre* [in the south-east]. *This was followed by two out of the three plays in their summer season, playing PC Nash in* The Sound of Murder *and Clayton in* House Guest. *After that I was cast to play in an open-air production of* Romeo & Juliet. *This would have been a fabulous continuation of the momentum created by the earlier jobs. Sadly this never came to fruition as the season was cancelled due to insufficient ticket sales… later I played my fourth policeman of the year.*

It's almost too painful to contemplate. You long for next year's letter to begin: 'Imagine my surprise when, out of the blue, Nick Hytner asked me to play Lear in the National's new production…'

But money can lead to interminable dullness too. One letter

starts well, but then descends into rather more than you might care to know about pension schemes:

> SEASONS' *greetings! The year began with my father recovering from the insertion of a pig's valve into his heart… one pension scheme (USS) announced that it was consulting its members on moving from a 1/80th to a 1/60th scheme. I hope they can implement this retrospective improvement in the next five years…*

Meanwhile a farmer feels that Yuletide is the perfect time to update all his friends on CAP support prices:

> SUGAR *beet (no acreage subsidy but a quota of 2,400 tonnes at a fixed price of around pounds 30 a ton)…*

Cars can also bring out the most tedious in so many people, some because they love them too well, and can talk the torque forever:

> DROPPING *the roof on the TVR and driving the cold roads for the hell of it. I am enjoying this. I really like the engine. Nothing clever, an OHV V6, 2.9 litres. It makes a lovely noise and that juicy fat torque makes for swift and easy driving…*

But the torque was evidently neither juicy nor fat enough:

> IN MAY *I sold the car. It was a great experience. Very much in the big Healey/TR3 mould and now a bit overlooked in the flood of MX5s and MGFs and later, more glam TVRs.*

Could one reader in a hundred make anything out of that? Others just like to keep you up to speed on every detail of their motoring lives:

> IN MAY, *en route to visit Tom's cousin Rhiannon and her husband in Taunton, the car started making funny noises, and to cut a long story short, we called the AA…*

Seven months later, they're filling us in on an engine fault! Why don't people realize that, unless they're talking about a canary yellow 1912 Rolls-Royce, we have very little interest in their vehicles? Few round robinners allow that to slow them down:

> JONTY *sold the Rover 214 to Nanette, who is the cook at the village school, with a comprehensive three-month guarantee.*

> TOM *now has a VW Polo GT 1991, dark grey in colour, with new alloy wheels and a large bore stainless steel exhaust.*

> TO HETTY'S *delight, she got a new car in July, a Mazda 323. She polishes it every other weekend.*

> MY PERIODS *seem to have stopped, at last. I'm overweight and hope that I don't gain any more. I have been looking for a camper van.*

Others feel a need to speak of their vehicles at even greater length. Here's a family from the East Midlands who travel widely — Cornwall, Wales and even France:

THIS YEAR we used our new van. This is my opportunity to say a bit more about it. After 30-odd years and two VW campers later, we expanded to a small motorhome (Autosleeper Talisman) which is a 4-berth with toilet / shower, cooker, fridge, heater and all the usual conveniences. This is based on the 2l petrol Talbot Express with a

GRP one-piece body (no leaks). I used my annual bonus to convert it to LPG (35p / l) and took it to Anglesey for the most competitive quote, and got a weekend in the Welsh mountains thrown in. I have made a list of future tweaks like turbo charger, air suspension, twin choke carb, power steering cruise control but these may have to wait a little longer.

This is from a family who spent Christmas in France:

ON New Year's Day it snowed and was bitterly cold, I had to go out and move my car, since all Lastide residents must park on the opposite side of the road every fifteen days, but the streets are so narrow that you have to wait until everybody else is ready to move and then do it together.

To recall a minor parking problem from twelve months previously argues a certain determination. But you might not believe that anyone would go so far as to use a Christmas letter to describe their TV viewing habits. In a way it's quite honest; most people are so busy describing their exhausting charity work, exotic holidays and artistic hobbies that they somehow don't get round to admitting that most of the time they're slumped in front of the box, like the rest of us. Not this London family, however:

> I'M SURE *you'll be relieved to learn that we are upholding the good name of the British TV viewing public. Last January we were recruited to BARB who record everything we watch on TV to put together the national statistics. For the first couple of days we thought we ought to just watch BBC4 all night long to keep up the intellectual standard but soon drifted back to watching the shopping channels... we earn a small remuneration for doing the service, and have clocked up about £50 so far. We are saving up for a set of knives.*

They go on to describe what seems to be almost all the programmes they've watched in the course of the year.

> THERE WAS *a feature on 'holding onto the electric fence' and seeing what happened, which brought back memories to Sally of walks with her family in the country and holding onto her dad who was holding onto a live fence...*

Digital viewers should press the red 'destruct' button now.

Politics rarely crops up in circular letters, and when you see what some people write you can understand why. This is from a Labour activist in Yorkshire.

> TASK *Number 1 has been to regroup and get ourselves geared up to start the climb back. Group agreed a major increase in the self-*

imposed levy immediately after the election to continue to fund
regular quarterly newsletters in the key parts of the district. We
are now distributing the third one since the election, which is
better than we did before I became leader, though we still have
some distribution and quality problems. I prepared a detailed
framework strategy for how we should seek to get back in, which has
been agreed by the district party, and we've commenced the branch
by branch initial audit of organization and activity which it
envisaged... I'm trying in effect to get a performance-managed
system in place that focuses effort in key areas...

This is just a small part of his description of what they get up to in
that Labour party. And people wonder why interest in the demo-
cratic process is declining! But, as with religion, people tend to
proselytize their political views. One man in the Midlands sends
a brief note about his year, including just two lines about his son's
marriage. This is accompanied by around 2,000 words attacking
the new European constitution and a postcard you can send to
Buckingham Palace:

THE QUEEN's *Chief Secretary, Sir Robin Janvrin, told us in May:*
'The Queen has asked to be regularly briefed on the number of
postcards being received.'

Oh yes, and this year she's taking her summer holiday in Faliraki.
My 'too much information' file is bulging with letters, though
some missives stand out as being quite spectacularly overlong.

One letter is forty densely typed pages, of which two are devoted to the arrival at his party of a stripogram girl dressed as a policeman. Another comes from a gay telecommunications executive and is arranged in chapters, as if it were work in progress on an autobiography. It consists of thirty-two crammed pages, of which fully four are devoted to his being stranded during a snowstorm – the gridlocked traffic, his good fortune in finding a hotel room, the need to abandon his car ('I moved it to a more prominent position in the car park, so that our security guard could keep an eye on it…') and the train journey back to London. There is also perhaps more than is strictly necessary about his close friendship with a young man he discovers selling the *Big Issue*. But nothing whatever in this man's life is too trivial to escape being mentioned:

THIS YEAR, *over lunch at the Dew Drop Inn, my Mum was bemoaning the fact that it is no longer possible to phone the local office of the Gas Board. Instead, one ends up speaking to someone in a Call Centre in Glasgow! Mum was saying, 'It was so much better when we could walk into the local gas office in Broadley.' At this point, the gentleman at the next table turned round and asked, 'Excuse me, did you mention Broadley? That is where I live!' In conversation, the gentleman told us he was chairman of the Broadley Historical Society. 'But,' I said, 'I thought Henry Cousins was chairman of the Broadley Historical Society!' The gentleman replied, 'I am Henry Cousins!'*

But the winner has to go to a most astonishing screed, published every year by an academic in Scotland, who sends it to, among others, all his former pupils. He calls this his 'general epistle' and I have been sent what he terms GE5. I estimate that it is 39,000 words – slightly longer than this book. Since it includes a substantial section on every student who has ever passed through his care, no doubt it is of interest to at least some of them. But the letter also includes his musings on cricket, the state of society in general, academic life, a whole page devoted to knotty parking problems, and a lengthy story concerning his landlord and a leaky roof. It is also one of the few letters to include a full page of notes for readers:

> BECAUSE *GE5 has been composed in bits over so long a period, some words of explanation are necessary. Refer to the foot of page 1 and the top of page 2 for the original plan of the structure. Sections 1 and 2 (pages 1 to 36), news of me and the University, were written as they now stand during the period June to August 2002 (though, as indicated in the opening paragraph of page 1, part of it had existed in an earlier version around Easter 2002... as you read these sections bear in mind that allusions in these sections to 'this session' refer to session 2001–02. The ensuing sections, 3a and 3b...*

Aargh! But we may not be alone in our frustration. A German reader, Ulrich Noetzel, wrote to tell me that the situation is desperate in his country too. He received a letter eight pages long, of which he was able to translate only a small part before falling into a deep, catatonic slumber (he doesn't actually write this, but I am sure it must be true).

> THIS circular continues the traditional sequence of the annual chronicle. It begins where the last one ended. Because only the highlights are related, one should remember that usually a year does not consist solely of highlights. Eighty per cent of the time we are at home in München-Gladbach. This circular concentrates on the other times.

Bring back that jigsaw!

The Pyramids (Overrated)
— and other tales from abroad

NEXT ONLY TO the dazzlingly successful children, the passages in round robins that most infuriate the recipients are those describing holidays. And there are so many. The British middle classes, more prosperous than ever before, with access to the cheapest air fares in Europe, and having seemingly endless free time at their disposal, travel more in a year than their parents probably did in a decade and their grandparents in a lifetime.

And they feel the need to describe these trips, often in the most excruciating detail. In the chapter entitled 'The Stubbed Toe Blackspot' there's a man who gives an account of his holiday virtually on an hour-by-hour basis. If this person were invited round to your house, and commandeered as much of your time to provide the same account orally, you would want to force dry bread down his mouth until he could no longer talk, or even move his jaw. Yet people seem to imagine that this is acceptable social behaviour if it takes the form of a letter.

But at least that person spent a perfectly ordinary holiday, of the kind that two thirds of his readers might be able to enjoy them-selves. Others, however, clearly regard the description of their vacations as a form of social climbing, such as this from west London:

THIS *is going to be a shorter letter than usual; we are preparing to go on a trip to Australia and New Zealand, later today... Travel, travel, travel seems to be the main theme of this year. In September we both went to New York on Concorde; we had flown on it the previous year, for the first time, and we had both fallen in love with it. When we learned it was going to be retired we were determined to fly on Concorde, possibly for the last time. In fact, we flew to New York, and flew back to London on Concorde and absolutely loved it! Since flying on Concorde we have become Concorde junkies... in New York we stayed at the Plaza Hotel, which is very plush. We had a week or so between Concorde flights, so decided to go to Niagara Falls.*

Life must seem pretty empty for them now, reduced to crawling across the sky at a mere 600 mph.

Here's a not untypical letter. You can imagine how a paragraph like this might make the wretched recipient want to track the writers down on holiday and taunt a gorilla into savaging them, or at least puncture their lilos:

JEREMY *has done so many air miles, he has attained premier status with BA!! It can come in handy, like when he was so held up getting to the airport he still caught the plane, despite arriving at LHR only 10 minutes before departure. We had three extra special trips. One to Uganda to visit Jen, and sat with mountain gorillas, AWESOME! One to Washington DC where I got to sit with John Glenn who was astute, fit, well and still flying his own plane, great to chat to someone who is a part of exciting history I can remember happening, and one in Rome where, due to having to leave early to catch a plane, instead of the group tour of the Vatican museum, Jeremy and I had a private escorted tour while the museum was closed to visitors. We do feel very privileged.*

That sounds a lot of travel. But it was not quite enough:

ON THE holiday front, we skied in January, spent a week on the Llangollen canal in summer, a long weekend at Center Parcs in Sherwood Forest (the best bit for me was carriage driving) and had a long sunny weekend with Pete and Paula in the Algarve.

It's hard to know which is more tedious – wearisome boasting or dejection. Here's a sample of each:

No sooner back, then off again to France with Tessie and Mungo, then to Wales with them to visit Tim, who breeds falcons for the Arab market. Then there was Easter, our own holiday in Tuscany, holiday in Brittany with Tessie, Jack and Seth, lazy summer days, and Mungo's baptism party. Off they went, back to UAE. So we had another holiday in Dorset to console ourselves!

Alternatively:

THE YORKSHIRE DALES *were not a huge success, as we didn't want to walk, and there wasn't a lot else on offer. We did our best, but we won't be returning.*

Others strain, perhaps a little too hard, to sound sophisticated:

OH NO, *not another Greek Island! How do we do it? By having a well-paid wife, that's how! Holidays this year included two weeks in Turkey on the side of a small bay, voted one of the best views in the world. Our second holiday took us to the Red Sea Riviera, where we went to see the Pyramids (overrated).*

Sometimes telling you what has happened is not enough. Some writers need to describe intricately what they plan to do in the near future.

FIRST *we fly to Samoa in the South Pacific before flying to Thailand via Auckland and Singapore. We plan to stay on Phuket Island for a few days before moving on to Bangkok. Sri Lanka is the next stop for 16 days and we hope to see most of the island during this time. From Colombo we fly home via Dubai for a few more rounds of golf before reaching Vienna for a short visit, and then home in time for Christmas. After spending New Year with family and friends, we plan to fly out to our house in Florida until mid-March. Plans for the end of next year will be developing whilst Winnie is working and we are playing golf.*

Can't wait for next year's letter!

The temptation to write too damn much is one that many people cannot resist. Reading some of the letters people send is like being invited round and then forced to look at every single one of their holiday snaps, while listening to a commentary on them all. ('Now this is a bit wobbly, I think I must have been standing on a rocky boulder when I took it, but you can probably see the little statuette of a saint, well they told us there was a fascinating story attached to that...') This next letter, probably fewer than 2,000 words all told, glances over their 'two splendid visits to the States' and a 'Caribbean idyll' before getting down to serious business in Spain and Portugal:

> FIRST *stop was Salamanca, a university town of golden stone with a delightful plaza mayor. (What better place to have* gambas al ajillo *for lunch followed by Ben & Jerry's after dinner, as bands of students strummed and sang to everyone's delight?) West into Portugal to Porto, centre of the port wine trade, with lodges lining the promenade of Villa Nova de Gaia across the Duoro River... south to Coimbra, old town, twelfth-century granite cathedral, university courtyard and clock and bell tower... exquisitely restored* azuelo *tiles depict the stories of La Fontaine's fables while the cloisters of the monastery of St Jerome commemorate Vasco da Gama's exploration... after sightseeing we feasted on* frango no espeto — *roasted chicken, no vegetables...*

Heavens, is it 9.30 already? I really should be getting home to bed.

No, no, I don't need the main course, watching my weight, you know...

Some people love names, and this is puzzling. Do they imagine that, even if all their recipients know who these people are, they have the faintest interest in their cat's cradle of meetings and trips? This letter, a chronological account of the sender's year, includes no fewer than twenty-nine different names, many repeated, in just two paragraphs.

JULY: *Tom and Jean spent a few days down in Frome with Theresa and later Tom stayed with Anne, and then went by train to Leicester, and stayed a week with Carrie. Meanwhile, while Jean gave a talk about St Francis to a Franciscan Day Centre in Norwich, Theresa and Jean visited Terry and Anita in their flat in Chippenham, and later in the month Jean led the Franciscan chapter meeting in Birmingham in her role as vice-minister for Dottie, who is ill. Pete has continued to visit Conrad daily. Conrad has moved to a nursing home. Later in the month we had a birthday picnic for Pete. We were joined by Carrie and all her family, Theresa and Duncan, Anne, Justin, and two of his boys, and Terry and Anita... Jacob stayed on with us, and we took him to the Nene Valley railway on his way home.*

The social whirl continues giddily:

AUGUST: *For our wedding anniversary we got a new carpet for the front room. It is a deep pink colour and looks lovely. We had a very*

happy day up near Diss with Jean's nephew Tom Parkinson and his
wife Jen and their two children Aeldred and Isolde. David and Pat
were there and we were joined by Claire and Rob and their two
daughters, Daisy and baby Emily, and by Dominic and his
Jacqueline. We missed John and Hettie as they had been held up.
We got back to the hospital to see Conrad, but he had died earlier
that evening. At his funeral we had the joy of seeing Gabriel, who
was over from Canada.

They must all wear name tags. 'Hi, I'm Flossie, and I married
Duncan's brother's wife's sister's best friend…'

It is amazing what sticks in people's minds. This letter comes
from a gay Anglican vicar, who sends a newspaper including
stories about his life:

CROWDS *gasped with shock in April when an Anglican priest fell*
for a mermaid. However, all was not as it seemed. During a post-
Easter break, the Rev. Patrick Brien eagerly made his way to the
statue of the Little Mermaid, intending to fulfil a lifelong ambition
to see the statue 'in the metal'. He was disappointed to discover that
there were yards of plastic barrier tape surrounding the area and
the huge cobblestones on the bankside were being replaced. This did
not seem to have discouraged other tourists, so Mr Brien followed
their example. Unfortunately a quantity of loose builder's sand
proved to be rather a slippery customer, and the good clergyman
found himself having a heavy and impromptu sit-down…

And so on and so forth, for quite a lot longer.

Other holidays are just baffling:

RENÉE *and I also had to pull out of the reunion marking the 39th anniversary of the 1964 student car trip to Petra and Jerusalem, which took place in Sligo.*

Sligo? Not exactly the rose-red city half as old as time.

And not everyone's holiday is perfect. Disasters come both great and small, though rarely too small to escape being recorded in true Pooter fashion.

WE VISITED *a small town, the name of which we have forgotten. Overcast skies changed to glorious sunshine, and I managed to order a meal at a street café, though I forgot the 'au lait' bit so we had black tea. They must have seen us coming as I thought 2 euros a cup a bit steep.*

BERTIE *was at a Chinese banquet in Beijing, and was seated between two male Chinese who only spoke Mandarin (and he's not even fluent in English!) He was using chopsticks very badly. They sought to be courteous and occasionally put food on his plate from the rotating glass servery in the centre of the table. He saw sea slugs on the plate and when they were near him, deciding British cunning was in order, he would quickly rotate the servery through 10 degrees so the slugs would pass him by. The courteous Chinese would have none of this. Sea slugs are a delicacy, and they both*

served him some. Of course they had to be eaten. The whole pile
of them.

Some catering establishments have a sign up saying something like: 'If you are dissatisfied, please tell us. If you are satisfied, please tell your friends.' This is not a dictum to which round robinners subscribe, preferring to store their gripes for months before releasing them on hundreds of people who will never be in a position to benefit:

> I DIDN'T *enjoy our summer holiday in Sicily as much as I ought,*
> *because the place we had chosen to stay was supposed to be 4*****
> *and it was not what we expected at all. The room stank of smoke*
> *(I did book a non-smoking room!) and the shower door kept falling*
> *off every time you used it – luckily we had already had our annual*
> *showers! Every time you sat on the toilet seat, you wobbled to one*
> *side and you thought you were going to end up on the floor. The*
> *food was average to poor, and we thought the four-star rating may*
> *have had Mafia connections.*

'I see we had a letter from the Whittles. Any news?' 'Not all good, I'm afraid. Apparently the Mafia arranged for them to have a wobbly toilet seat on holiday...'

Other people suffer more considerable inconveniences:

> WE HAD *a scare after a holiday flight in March when I had a*
> *funny feeling in my leg and was sent there as a DVT suspect (false*

alarm) and then in June Phil decided to have a 'Beckham' injury and broke a meta-tarsal in his left foot. This was incurred not by any athletic pursuit, but by falling down a hidden animal hole while on holiday in France... we had another holiday, in Gran Canaria, where I'd booked an apartment in a small resort via the Internet. The picture on the net turned out to be as accurate as an 'artist's impression' in a brochure, and the apartment was in the middle of a building site.'

And others suffer even greater disasters. This is from a decidedly grumpy letter:

ARTHUR *had a mild heart attack during a visit we made to gardens just off the M4 to see the spectacular display of red, yellow, mauve, white and chestnut stemmed shrubs. He lay on a bank of snowdrops while a medic administered oxygen before an ambulance took him to hospital in Bristol. He had an interesting week there with Loyd Grossman specified meals. His slow recovery now gives him a good excuse for avoiding social gatherings...*

So we won't be meeting him soon. We can live with that.

With holidays, it seems that all our writers are either glass half-empty or glass half-full people. Some clearly skirt over anything that goes wrong. Others love to dwell on every mishap.

WE WENT *on a cruise to the Canaries while the kitchen got finished, but that was our first poor cruise — the trip to Morocco*

was cancelled because of terrorism and Madeira because of storms —
the QE2 which should also have been there docked beside us in
Tenerife instead — the weather was cold and windy all week while
England was enjoying a heat wave. The last two days all shops,
museums etc. were closed as it was Maundy Thursday and Good
Friday. Luckily we had a really good two-week cruise in August —
Italy, Greece, Slovenia. Unfortunately at the end, Roderick fell
badly on a steep gravelled road in Rhodes and broke his glasses and
got a magnificent black eye and lots of bruises and pulled muscles
which took weeks to heal.

Going on a cruise is simply to tempt disaster. Take this male
traveller. Nothing actually went wrong with the voyage itself, but:

THE BOAT was chock-a-block, with too many elderly widows on the
prowl, lascivious lips all aquiver, slobbering at the jaws, while
emitting lecherous snorts and grunts.

That sounds rather like fun. The cruise line should quote him in
the brochure.

Or take this, from someone who sounds like a serious grump:

PERHAPS our most memorable events of the year have been our trips
abroad, one of which was disastrous. We decided to spend Christmas
and New Year in Italy and set off as soon as term finished. By the
time we had reached the halfway point of our journey, it was
apparent that I had a serious dose of influenza. We carried on to

our destination, a village 50 miles south of Turin, where Amelia's mother now lives. On arrival, I tumbled into bed where I lay with a fever for the next eight days. It was so bad that I even went to see an Italian doctor, who examined me, chastised me for not wearing a vest, and told me I had an enlarged liver. New Year's Eve was spent watching on Italian TV the incredibly duff celebrations taking place at all major cities throughout the country.

Luckily, on his return to England a real doctor – i.e. not an Italian one – tells him there is nothing wrong with his liver. Phew.

Some people have nothing but bad luck. This family had no fewer than three holidays, all of which went dreadfully wrong:

AFTER moving mother into her new flat, Maurice and I had a short break in Guernsey at a 4-star hotel overlooking the sea. Our weekend of luxury was something of a disappointment, with two of the three gourmet restaurants being closed or fully-booked, so we had to eat in a makeshift dining room by the swimming pool with the heady aroma of chlorine wafting by. Our romantic breakfasts on the balcony had to be shared with the decorators… our next major event was mother's birthday present, a cruise to Norway and the Arctic Circle at the end of June. Off we went to the Land of the Midnight Sun. Life being what it is, we barely saw the sun at all for two whole weeks and certainly not at midnight. We experienced fog and torrential rain… having had one cold, wet holiday and one where the facilities weren't up to scratch, after Maurice's mother's funeral we decided we needed a break. Due to shortage of funds we opted to stay in a friend's caravan in the south of France, and though we knew the facilities would be 'basic' we thought in September we'd be guaranteed good weather. How very foolish!

Some people are just never pleased:

IN AUGUST *we went on holiday to Morocco together — to Club Med. It was Luke's first encounter with Club Med and he was quite taken aback that at those high prices he was expected to serve himself at dinner! He also hated the shrieking microphones. For me it was a final goodbye to Club Med. The hectic, self-destructive life, together with the exploitation and the phoniness hit me more forcefully than it had ever done before.*

These people went to Holland to see the bulb fields:

IN AMSTERDAM *we found ourselves billeted in a seedy hotel — cigarette burns on dirty sheets and a greasy spoon restaurant — adjacent to a Sex Museum and lap-dancing bar in front of which a thong-clad (and not much else!) full-bosomed wench touted for custom even in broad daylight amongst the junkies and the drug-peddlers who throng the main street... so on to the bulbfields — which turned out to be acres of bare earth since they'd lopped off all the heads of the bulbs the week before our arrival.*

This is from a man who had a trip to Northumberland. His 'Most Romantic Moment' came when he played the flute to himself on Hadrian's Wall:

> FOLLOWED *promptly by the Least Romantic Moment of 2003.*
> *I stood up: my trousers didn't. They were caught on the stones, and*
> *the bottom fell out of my world. About a mile back to the car, past*
> *the tourists hooting happily, my neb in the air all the way. No other*
> *trousers in the car. My coffee breaks on the way home were in the*
> *dingiest, most ill-lit places I could find.*

To avoid confusion: the *OED* says that 'neb' is northern dialect for a nose.

This next is from a couple who plan to go and live in Greece.

> OUR COMMAND *of the Greek language is progressing slowly,*
> *though our incident with the camper van window tested our*
> *knowledge to the limit. After we'd managed to ease our way into the*
> *van with a lump hammer, we then had to negotiate getting a*
> *replacement window at a local garage. We got there eventually*
> *through a mixture of mime and pidgin Greek. However, we later*
> *learned that the Greek word for 'glass' is exactly the same as the*
> *word for 'mosque' except the accent is in a different place.*

For some people you can only feel sorry. These people had planned the photographic holiday of a lifetime in New Zealand:

I CAME *home with 1,200 photos, many of which were ruined,*
because a piece of mohair off my sweater got caught invisibly
behind the camera's mirror. My other camera leaked in light due
to the foam seal on the back cover having rotted. Yes, I had checked
for faults before I left home.

You can usually find a 3-for-2 offer on Boots' disposables; might
be safer next time.

Other people naturally tempt danger:

JOHN *joined an expedition to Cho Oyu, the sixth highest*
mountain in the world, only 2,000 ft lower than Everest, and no
oxygen. It turned out to be a difficult and hazardous trip owing to
the atrocious weather. John was one of three chosen for the summit
attempt, but did not quite make it owing to severe neck pain. (A
blow from a football at base camp had aggravated on old injury.)
At advanced base camp, there were two other groups of whom two
Germans and the leader of an Australian group died of altitude
sickness and two other Australians had to be rescued by helicopter.
In John's party one went down lower following a heart attack, one
with kidney stones and a Sherpa with altitude sickness. On his
return to Kathmandu, John learned that six people had been killed
by an avalanche where he had recently been.

One letter is basically an extended account of a yachting trip in
which everything goes wrong. Here is a flavour:

AT THIS POINT *the engine died completely. We were towed into harbour where our passports were confiscated.*

You'd think France would be fairly safe. You would be mistaken.

FREJUS *was so hot we could hardly move, quite apart from being hemmed in by the forest fires, many of which were started deliberately, that you may recall gutted large parts of France. The campsite down our road was completely burned out on our first night, and at times the fires were too close for comfort. Still, in good British tradition we sat on our patio in summer gear, supping red wine and sampling local cheeses while ash fell from the sky like snow!*

Occasionally those who are lucky enough to live somewhere nice invite their readers along. Not necessarily with great enthusiasm.

GREG, *Petra, Shelley and James wish you all a very happy festive season, a very happy Christmas and the best of health and luck for the next year, and if you come to Jersey we will get to know about it, so you might as well advise us. Our impression, as a tourist place, it is not great value for money. Great beaches, good scenery, but lacks a focal point, and hotels are poor quality and expensive.*

Others are slightly more welcoming:

MARGERY'S *legacy allowed us to buy a delightful holiday home on the Devon coast. Do come and stay!*

But the writer nervously realizes that this might be taken as an invitation to stay for free, and adds: 'very reasonable rates!'

This next must be one of the most disastrous holidays ever recorded in a round robin. The writer lives on the south coast, and he and his wife had used a local paper offer of £5 trips across the Channel.

> SENSIBLE *crossing, no alcohol, arrive in France at noon local time. To the Market Square for our first couple of drinks, on to a restaurant for lunch. Visit a couple of bars on our way back to the boat, and we're in the mood for a few more in the bar on the return crossing. Now the reason the offer was so cheap was that it was end of season. Bar stocks run down, so no beer or wine…*

The writer, Dave, buys six tonics from the bar and a bottle of vodka from the duty free.

> YOU KNOW *what it's like when you're pouring your own? You've got it, not exactly optic measures! After a while, Dave decides he needs a walk. Next thing, Daph is being called by tannoy to the information desk, only to be told that Dave has had a serious fall and cut his head rather badly. We are met at the terminal by an ambulance and taken to hospital. While waiting for his head and face to be stitched, soaked in blood, Dave constantly asks for the whereabouts of his bag containing passport, camera, phone etc. Eventually Daph can take no more and decides to go home. In her wisdom she unfortunately slips, falls and breaks her hip.*

She is taken to the same hospital her husband is in, but he, panicked about her disappearance, has discharged himself and has to be tracked down by the police and returned to hospital.

> AFTER *a short while Daph and Dave realize they are in adjacent beds. The nursing staff are in stitches (!) Daph is taken to a ward for an operation, and allowed home one week later with the aid of a Zimmer frame.*

Eventually the bag containing passport etc. is found by a marine worker who lives 100 yards from the hospital.

> WHEN *Mike collected the bag it also contained the vodka. Looking at the amount left now we understand what led to our 'downfall'.*

Well, that letter has two virtues, unlike most of the others. It isn't boasting about the writers' wealth, sophistication or resourcefulness, and it even tells an interesting story. Here is a holiday that ended in precisely the opposite fashion, though it too is sad in its way:

> WE ALSO *had a trip to Le Touquet — we must have been the only car returning to the UK with empty bottles clinking in the boot, due to almost missing the ferry and the presence of an over-enthusiastic recycler.*

The Cat that Could Open the Fridge

'THIS HAD US wiping away tears of mirth,' says one reader of a letter included here. It's a long list of accidents and mishaps that occurred to a distant relative living in Australia. They had never met this person, and presumably that is one reason why his endless misfortunes seem so hilarious. People – good, kind people – people who would never dream of laughing if they knew the victim, find themselves rocking and chortling and hugging themselves with delight when it refers to someone they don't know and probably never will.

But it's not merely that we have the capacity to be heartless when we have no connection with the person involved. There is something inherently comical about people who feel the need to describe every misfortune, great or small, that life has sent their way. These people always look on the dark side of life. The effect is cumulative. It's like an old slapstick film. A man falls off the back of a lorry, then is knocked over by a car and drops into a puddle, and the audience – the same people who would rush to help if they saw it happen in real life – laugh their heads off. Take the letter from which this book took its title. The writer lives in Devon. It needs to be quoted at some length to convey the full, rich, tragic effect.

As EARLY *as last November my GP was worried by the high Creatinine level in my blood, indicating kidney problems. Several private consultations were funded by insurance including a kidney biopsy in March which confirmed scarring and damage due to blood pressure that was too high for my body. Pills reduced that, so I was OK for my hip operation.*

Already readers may feel that this is more than they strictly need to know. But the writer is hardly into his stride.

The MOVEMENT *of my left hip had deteriorated in a year and X-rays in March showed the surfaces of both joints were very rough. The consultant confirmed that there was no sideways rotation of either hip and he agreed to do both together, urgently! In May, before I had the operation, I had to have help with socks and shoelaces but still managed to walk and dance up to the last week, provided I had had some pills. During the op, there was too much bleeding from the first hip so only one was done… in fact my new hip dislocated twice, which meant that I had three general anaesthetics in ten days! The drugs were fine and I had no problems except with Codeine, which caused a bad turn of constipation for a couple of days.*

The writer devotes 930 words of the letter, perhaps two-fifths of the total, to this account of his and his wife's medical problems. It contains many cliffhangers and several false dawns.

By EARLY AUGUST, *I thought I was doing well. However a routine blood test showed the Creatinine was back, and more importantly, I had a very high calcium level. At 10 o'clock the GP said he would fax the consultant and at 2 p.m. I had a call to say there was a hospital bed waiting! I went on a drip straight away, as I was severely dehydrated. Within a few days I was feeling fine and eating everything I could get.*

By now it would be almost disappointing to believe that he was getting any better. Luckily for his muse, he wasn't.

HOWEVER, *the full diagnosis took three weeks of many tests, scans, another kidney biopsy, and a spleen biopsy, which is rather risky but went well… once they decided I have Sarcoid, large doses of steroid were prescribed. Sarcoid is a dysfunction affecting the lymph glands, and can produce a wide variety of symptoms. It seems likely I have had it for several years… I take five different pills a day, with an additional one on Sundays. Aspirin is included, to thin my blood — small knocks make me bleed or bruise. My second hip replacement is due in March.*

Just when you think things can't get any worse, the whirligig of fate turns upon his wife.

SONIA'S *right knee worried me last December as she suffered considerably, then it seemed better in spring, after a fall. During August, she broke a toe by shutting her right foot in the car door.*

> *In September we both saw consultants and got clearance that I*
> *could fly off somewhere. A late booking gave us a nice week on*
> *Jersey, until the last evening, when at a Scottish dance, Sonia fell*
> *over. She had to drive back to the hotel that evening, and to the*
> *airport and home the next day. An X-ray confirmed a broken*
> *bone… three days later she had the much-postponed minor*
> *operation on her right knee, which confirmed the considerable wear*
> *and tear she had. Next she had a nasty spell of sciatica…*

That provides just a flavour of their medical problems. The year begins to improve, though bad luck, like an unwanted stray dog, continues to snap at their feet. They ride on the London Eye, but it rains. Next:

> GOING *to work on one of her few days this year, the car broke*
> *down but S managed to drift into a lay-by. The battery has to be an*
> *expensive special, as it is under the driver's seat and must not give*
> *off fumes. Then one day at the supermarket, the electronic key died,*
> *so that was another £90! The runabout I had been driving needed*
> *a tarpaulin to keep the damp out of the electrics…*

Disasters, great and small, continue.

> THIS YEAR *Jenny bought a new lounge carpet, but the fitters*
> *dropped oil in the doorway… Ben managed to fall off the porch*
> *roof in September and is still waiting for a decision on treatment*
> *for a broken wrist.*

Not quite all is gloom, though. Relatives from Canada arrive. A new computer works well. The children are flourishing, for the most part. But then the letter limps on to its tragic conclusion.

> THIS YEAR *Snugs (Mr Snugglekins, our cat) has kept us on our toes.*

(The ones that weren't mangled in the car door, presumably.)

> HE HAS *learned how to open the door of our new large fridge…*

This is the point, on reading the letter, that one is inclined to burst into wholly unfair, entirely inappropriate, and utterly hysterical laughter. On top of all their appalling medical problems, the rain, the malfunctioning car keys, the oil on the new carpet, and every misery and horror that has blighted their lives for twelve whole months, they are faced with every cat- or dog-owner's worst imaginable nightmare – the pet that can help itself!

One reader has sent in a letter cherished since it arrived in 1990. This too is a seemingly endless list of medical misfortune. To give you just a flavour:

> HIP *operation and also the prostate op… very bad flu so I was too ill and too infectious for Tom to visit… back in hospital, in traction, for Christmas and the New Year… I coughed and wheezed with pleurisy and could not get rid of the deep infection in my lung, the doctor had me X-rayed and there was a patch on it! It took four lots of antibiotics over five months for it to clear up…*

*after Tom's prostate op they found cancer cells, and the surgeon
recommended another operation… we both felt better by mid-May
but I suddenly developed what turned out to be an acute attack of
diverticulitis (at the time we had no idea what the ghastly pain
could be)… bone scan… arthritis brewing up… rheumatics really
rather ghastly.*

But their cup of woe was not yet full. After this long letter, in
which only one paragraph is devoted to non-medical news, the
writer adds:

WE ARE *still reeling over the dreadful way in which Margaret
Thatcher was called on to resign. We think it was ghastly treatment
after all she has done for us…*

But not, perhaps, quite as much as your doctors have done.

After all this it's a relief to find this one paragraph in an otherwise wonderfully chirpy letter from North Yorkshire:

AFTER *a brief respite last year, Angela's work situation seems to go
from bad to worse. The least said, the better.*

But some people clearly relish the opportunity for a good, long,
pipe-clearing, annual whinge. This letter is from a barrister who,
in spite of his misfortune, writes from an expensive address in
one of south-east England's most expensive towns. The second
sentence of his letter begins:

> MY *outstanding fees continue unabated and are still around*
> *£200,000. The pressure from my present Chambers was bad in*
> *the first part of the year, but eased later on… my new Internet*
> *Chambers are doing almost nothing to fetch my greater fees in*
> *and the lack of money is becoming a serious problem. My new*
> *American Chambers have not made the impact this year that*
> *I expected…*

And a Happy New Year to you, too! But this man's life goes on, from dreadful to appalling:

> THE MEDICAL *profession have continued their trail of havoc*
> *and destruction across every path I tread. They nearly killed*
> *the daughter of one of my pupils through a crass and inept*
> *misdiagnosis… they nearly killed the wife of one of my colleagues*
> *by stuffing her full of painkillers instead of realizing that she was*
> *developing septicaemia; luckily the truth came out before they*
> *orphaned a six-month-old baby.*

Several similar medical disasters are just averted, or else in some cases end in death. But his life is not all pain. He gives a paper at an important legal conference:

> I WAS *very pleasantly surprised at how well my paper was received.*
> *It is several years since I have had eminent university professors*
> *queuing up to congratulate me on my academic work!*

However, such moments are mere glimmers in the dark forest of his life. Later in the letter he describes trying to take his mother to the conference and finding it impossible to get across the road into the college from a bus stop. This account goes on for approximately five times the length he devotes to his triumph at the lecture podium and ends, after travails which would have driven Ulysses to despair:

> I KNEW *we were in the cheaper accommodation, but I had not bargained on the communal facilities extending to there being no wash-basins in our rooms, nor a bar of soap in the entire flatlet and the fact that the light outside the bathroom needed a new bulb and nobody had done anything about it...*

It takes a certain heroic persistence to recall a missing bar of soap five months after the event. But our correspondents know all about persistence. This is the letter from Australia which had the recipient wiping away the tears of laughter:

> TERRY *had his two-yearly colonoscopy. They removed two polyps, but found his diverticular was inflamed, so he had to have antibiotics for it, he was also going to a physio for a backache when he fell on the brick pavement in the garden, breaking his right hip (he had been up the ladder clearing away the guttering, came in for coffee, then went out to prune shrubs, and fell). We went by ambulance to the private hospital not far from home, but because he takes Warfarin they could not operate til the Friday... at the*

end of August we were just getting back to some type of normal life when Terry fell on the tiled floor in the kitchen, did not break anything, nasty cut on the corner of the eye and huge bruises and lumps on both knees due to Warfarin... We do not entertain any more, used to enjoy the odd little dinner parties, we just have tea or coffee and biscuits. I cannot walk very far because of my back problem when trying to nurse Mother when she broke her hip, which she never got over.

What is curious is that amid this medical mayhem, the writer still finds time to complain that the recycling team no longer comes round to take away the newspapers. Australia certainly seems to harbour a lot of poorly people. Occasionally they can blend news of their ailments in with tidings of the wider world:

During the year I have suffered from a prolapsed lumbar disc, osteoporosis, crumbling vertebrae, bronchitis, colonoscopy, endoscopy (under anaesthesia), low blood levels, low iron levels... other events of this year have included the introduction of a 10 per cent goods and services charge, equivalent to VAT.

From Canada comes a letter bringing yet more medical distress. After a page of gore, including internal bleeding, CAT scans and stomach ulcers:

I only use my dentures for looks now, because I'm unsure if they will stay put. So I don't go out in public much.

Back in Britain, there are fresh horrors. This man got food poisoning, which set off a chain reaction of blood poisoning, fits, a heart attack, pneumonia and cardiogenic shock.

> THE LATTER *is awkward! After being in hospital for another two weeks, Don's recovery is regarded locally as being quite miraculous. Full recovery after such an episode is not possible, and there is some permanent damage. He can recall nothing of the 25 days when he was in intensive care on life-support, nor the week previous to the hospital admission. Shirley, Douglas and Sal remember it very well, of course. During all this they were not encouraged to believe in his survival... Don was soon back at the Citizens' Advice Bureau. He also chairs our Wildlife and Local History Group.*

Or take this letter:

> LAST *February I had a sudden bout of gastroenteritis and lost two stone in ten days, living on ginger ale and peanut butter sandwiches, when I was able to keep anything down.*

Whoa there, too much sharing!

This next writer suffers from depression, which leads him to impulsive acts:

> I DROVE *and drove and drove until I found myself in Lowestoft. I thought, 'this is stupid. I'd better go home'. So I did.*

Others blend grief and gladness seamlessly:

MUM *is suffering from psoriasis on her scalp. They celebrated fifty-seven years of marriage this year.*

So many people seem to take pleasure in their own misfortunes, and pass them round in the way that others share favourite recipes.

THIS YEAR *has not been a very good one for the family healthwise. I started the ball rolling by passing out in a chair and being hospitalized for a week. Justin then had an abscess on his appendix, closely followed by Julian who had pneumonia… Alice has started a journalism course and has already had articles published on a local radio website (she had to give up Equine Studies as she became allergic to horses).*

This is from quite a short letter, but they certainly manage to pack it full of misery:

THE YEAR *didn't start at all well. For us the New Year was worse than usual because we are not devotees of cold, wet, frosty, foggy, snowy and windy weather… we bought a new car, a Fiat Punto, which generally goes well. Instead it didn't go well, and we had to take it back as it was misfiring due to a fuel injection fault. We had just got over this little hiccup when, two days later, the sound of running water was heard and the central heating header tank was found to have a crack in it… we went off to Scotland in the middle of May and experienced a fortnight of rain with only three days of fine weather. We took the car and caravan to the Outer Isles, but*

£600 *is really too expensive, and it does beg the question, all
things considered, as to whether Scotland really does want tourists
to come and spend money, because we encountered more boorish
behaviour than we have ever encountered previously . . . Derek's
blood pressure began to rise to 150/100 and at the end of the year
is still high, in spite of beta-blockers . . . downers have included the
new Fiat, which has performed unsatisfactorily, the agents even
more so, Scottish weather and some of the natives, a lot of people
passing a away within a very short time, and the quite unnecessary
public inquiry into the diversion of a well-known and well-used
bridleway in the parish.*

The letter ends:

ON THIS *note, we wish you an equally contented and peaceful
2004.*

Which sounds more sarcastic than they probably meant.

Meanwhile some people's children do the suffering on their
behalf:

BEN *saw a string of specialists as by now he was experiencing
urological problems and no one could say if the symptoms were
related. To date he has seen an orthopaedic specialist, a urologist
and a neurologist, has had several scans, physiotherapy, osteopathy
and seen a chiropractor, and everyone is stumped. He is very limited
in what he can do; heat is the only thing which alleviates the*

pain... to cap it all his girlfriend decided she couldn't cope with it all, and finished with him in the autumn. This really was the last straw... thankfully Rose ditched her boyfriend who was causing us so much trouble last year... alas, her friend from Grenada has turned out not to be such a good pal, as she is extremely lazy around the house. At the end of the summer Aime went to the doctor complaining of bad headaches, and was diagnosed as extremely anaemic. She is on iron tablets, but as she is a vegetarian, that doesn't help... Jacqui is still working at the Institute, but it failed to get university status after a poor subject review some time ago. All of her department is going to be involved in another move soon to a converted mill, which they are very unsure about as most of the building will be open plan with very little natural light.

Oh, give us a break, you yearn – quite unfairly – to sigh. Though for some people you really do feel sorry:

THIS YEAR'S main stress has been my neighbours' wind chimes. I can hear them clearly in my bedroom, even with the window closed. It drives me mad. My neighbours do not respond to polite requests, they will not take part in mediation and they are merely indignant at letters from the Council. I am a Quaker and a pacifist, I have training in conflict resolution – well, now I have first-hand knowledge too. I have discovered what hate is, and that I was blessed in not hating anyone for the first 33 years of my life.

And he had a viral infection for four months, including the Christmas period.

It's hard not to sympathize with this chap too:

> ROSIE *had read me some articles in the paper about people who divorce to live with an 'Internet lover'. We were amazed at what seemed to us unbelievable behaviour. Little did we know what lay ahead for us. During October, Rosie found herself chatting on the Internet for hours to a man in the USA. When the relationship came to an end, she was devastated as she had been infatuated with him. We had always felt that our marriage was 'a dream come true' and she swore she would never do it again. She tried hard to stop by removing her software...*

Which sounds like some ghastly sexual euphemism...

> BUT *she cried and reinstalled the software. On 13 August she left me, and two days later asked for a divorce to go and be with a man in Toronto. In March this year she went to Canada and married Arthur! She has not returned to the UK since. The grief experienced by her mother, my daughters, my parents, not to mention myself, is unimaginable. The physiotherapy practice had to be sold to meet the divorce settlement, and the house remortgaged. And I was left with our two cats.*

This is from the US:

DAVID *went to his 20th high school reunion this year and returned to tell me that our marriage was over. He and his high school sweetheart saw each other across the room and their long lost love was instantly rekindled… that he should find someone else sexually attractive causes me self-esteem problems that I thought had been worked out after years in therapy. The pain is almost physical. He was my third husband and I his second wife, but our souls were connected. I am trying to be strong, and like the phoenix rising, I will make my way through this…*

This next letter begins with the death of the (female) writer's mother, and continues in the same vein.

BEFORE *I went up to Mum's we had a visit from my girlfriend Emily who lives in the US. She had come over because her elderly aunt who lived in Warrington was very ill in hospital. Emily arrived at Heathrow and then travelled up to Warrington. I was going to Wigan myself to see Mum and Dad and spend some time with Emily a few days later. (Wigan is only a few miles from Warrington.) We met up a couple of times but saw little of each other because of spending time in different hospitals visiting our relatives. Emily then changed her return flight to the US as her aunt was still very ill, but then there was talk of her aunt being discharged to a nursing home, and Emily rebooked her flight. She boarded the train at Warrington, intending to spend the night at our home in Harrow before catching a flight home the next day.*

I was, of course, still in Wigan. Sadly, when she got off the train at
Watford, she was met by Richard who told her that her aunt had
died as she had boarded the train in Warrington. So, as you see,
not a good year.

You can say that again. But it was not over yet:

BETTY *had a dreadful accident during our visit to South Africa,*
but I am happy to say she has made a splendid recovery... We went
to Majorca for a week, but oh dear, the weather was unbelievable!
We were there for just over a day when the storms started. Wind,
rain, flash floods, you name it, we got it, and it continued like that
for the length of our stay... Tolstoy (our cat) is getting more frail.
He never really recovered from his broken leg last year and when he
began to lose weight, the vet diagnosed a liver tumour.

The most extraordinary thing about this list of horrors is that it is
decorated with little pictures of jolly Santas.

Sometimes people are just too fastidious to describe their
disasters in full:

TWO DAYS *prior to Sally's departure on an exciting trip to Latin*
America, we were visited by two policemen at midnight with the
truly awful news that Robert's brother Andrew had strayed from
hospital and had been killed outright by a road-sweeper.

There is no mention of whether the road-sweeper was a person or
a vehicle.

This is also slightly baffling:

> SO, *apart from Tom's ear, Matthew's kidney, my broken nose, and Fred's castration, it's been a good year. Fred has made an excellent recovery and hasn't actually noticed that anything is missing.*

We assume that Fred is a pet of some kind. But we are not told.

In some cases, you suspect that more is being hidden than revealed:

> WE HAD *an interesting New Year last year with one of my best friends ending up in hospital for a week after a 'domestic' with her boyfriend of the moment. I hope this year's won't be quite as exciting. Jerry spent the early hours of New Year's Day sitting in the kitchen armed with a golf club when the boyfriend went AWOL.*

And what on earth is this about?

> JULY *and August were incredibly hot, and on the 21st, right on cue, the potato crisp hullabaloo broke out, since when the village has been at various times in an uproar, pitting brother against brother, and we still await a decision from the planning authority.*

In this otherwise detailed letter, there is absolutely nothing to say what the potato crisp hullabaloo might be.

It is clear that for some people, misery is the only thing that keeps them going. One letter from the Midlands records in detail the anti-tumour drugs the writer, a woman, has been taking. Her cat dies, but there is consolation in the shape of a visit to Coventry. She has to give up working in her neighbour's garden, and can no longer make jam for her favourite charity. Her husband turns out to have Crohn's disease and ulcerative colitis. She ends:

> MOST *of my friends are suffering from serious illnesses, or looking after others. I hope the New Year brings ease to the suffering.*

Here is another letter which is almost, if not quite as terrible as the one from the man whose cat could open the fridge. It begins:

> DEAR FRIENDS, *well Christmas is here again, folks, and for us it's got to be an improvement on the one we had last year. We had an awful time with me having been ill since the previous May. Christmas Day turned out to be no exception, and we were glad when it was all over.*

But there is a chink of hope for these people – only a chink:

> FOR *the feline lovers, I am pleased to say that we still have our cat Noodles, but I won't say too much as our previous three cats didn't last long. The first was shot by an air rifle, the second was run over on Christmas Day 1999, and the last one died of leukaemia. The boys were heartbroken.*

The Hairy Archbishop

I DON'T WANT to make fun of anyone's religious beliefs, though it is amazing how many people feel the need to share theirs with everyone they write to. It must be a problem for religious folk. If you truly believe that those who, unlike you, have not been saved are slated for eternal damnation, then the very least you can do is bring them the good news about our Saviour. On the other hand, people who don't share your convictions are liable to ignore the rest of your letter, or even mock your testimony and avowals.

And it is certainly true that God moves in some mysterious ways. Take the woman from near Bristol who recounted this remarkable story to her friends:

MY *daughter-in-law has been healed of her dreadful eating intolerances. The doctors in the London hospital who have been trying to fathom out the reason for the problem have no answer to what has happened to her. A member of her church told Kimberley that she should visit a church in Bridlington, about eighteen miles from her home. She drove up on her own after a telephoned appointment was made and the vicar and a member of his congregation prayed for her. There was no immediate feeling of any change, but as she drove home again she felt very excited and*

very hungry and stopped in a filling station shop. She bought an
Eccles cake, which is something she had not eaten for years, but just
fancied as soon as she saw it. The wheat alone in it should have
been enough to put her in a coma, but she had no reaction at all.
Since then she has eaten everything she desired... her next step is
to try for a baby so we would value your prayers for that to happen.

Well, if God can manifest His purposes through loaves and fishes, He should be able to work miracles with a petrol-station Eccles cake. And the baby should be a doddle. Later in the same letter, the writer records that her son has been given funding for his youth work in Yorkshire.

FOR *three years starting last September he had several nail-biting*
weeks after not knowing what would happen. His attitude was that
if God wanted him there the funding would become available, and
his faith was rewarded.

The general idea seems to be that everything good that happens can be credited to God. But He is in no way to blame for anything that goes wrong. He is there to see you through the bad times. It doesn't seem to cross any of our writers' minds that if He can help you get better, He could presumably prevent you from getting ill in the first place. Or having that nasty accident.

This is from a British family based in the US:

SHAUN *has continued to be used by God in the places he serves: fire
department, church, state government and home... the Lord is
using Lucy's gifts through the church, and it is so exciting for me to
see. She has also been involved, along with Darren, in door-to-door
evangelism this term and she really enjoys that. She has new talents
as a puppeteer for the children's ministry at church. Who knew our
shy girl could do all these things in public?... So this has been a
remarkable year for us. We feel like the Lord has blessed us over and
over again. I don't write all this in any way to brag, but only to
give the Lord glory for all the ways He's touched our lives through
those who have encouraged, taught, befriended and helped us. And
to give Him praise for the sights he showed us, the prayers He
answered regarding our children and our lives, the strengths He
developed in us and the lessons he taught us. We are truly grateful
for His grace in our lives! May his blessings surround you!*

The fact that the poor door-to-door evangelist Darren suffered
from a severe case of mononucleosis '(glandular fever to you back
in England)' is skated over very briefly.

But illness never seems to dent anyone's faith. Quite the
opposite:

FOR *some years now Cynthia has been suffering from unpleasant
dizzy spells... at the end of 2002 her GP requested various tests
because the dizziness was getting worse. She had a brain scan in
February, and sadly this revealed that she has a non-malignant*

tumour of the brain. It is in a very difficult place, inside a fold of
the meninges, and the consultant would rather not operate if at all
possible. There is no treatment Cynthia can have because of the site
of the tumour, and so she has to adapt her life to coping with the
side effects. We are so very grateful for our total faith in a loving
and wise God.

Often writers do not see how their assertions of faith must seem
oddly juxtaposed with what happens to them:

DEAR friends, our Christmas wish for you this year is still the
same. Good health, happy days for you and your families, and the
sure knowledge of God's amazing and ever available love and peace
in your lives... Pru finally got her pain and sleepiness diagnosed as
polymyalgia overlying fibromyalgia. The first half of the year was a
sort of blur.

This is from the north of England:

THROUGH all our changes this year, we have known and felt
God's unchanging love and faithfulness, and He has helped us
through the difficult times. The hardest thing to accept has been the
sudden death of Rose's father in July, following a stroke. It was such
a shock, as he had been so active with no sign of ill-health and
Mum and Dad had only been with us a few days before he
collapsed.

Or take this, from the West Country:

WE *have been in a continuing haze of thanksgiving. Let me explain. For those who have not heard, Charles had a serious heart attack during the night last December, and was rushed to hospital. An angiogram showed a major blockage in an artery so he was transferred to a specialist unit where he had a tube (stent) insertion to re-open the valve and repair the damage… our most grateful thanks to everyone for the loving prayers, phone calls and support. THEY HELPED US BOTH SO MUCH!*

A Midlands family offer an alphabetical account of what seems to have been rather a mixed year, including:

B is for Borthwick Free Church. We continue to be blessed by increased numbers and faithful ministry.

G is for Grandma. She is as lively and cheerful as ever, in spite of her pain and disability from the arthritis and the muscle pain she feels. She can now ride to Tesco's on her Porsche-like scooter.

I is for Ikea [how did that get in?]

L is for Loss. In March we lost an elderly friend of ninety-four whom Sue had cared for through her involvement with the Tuesday fellowship. His funeral was a glorious opportunity to share the way that he had trusted The Lord as his Saviour in his last years.

M is for the Men's Convention. Stuart and forty others from church joined 4,300+ men at the Royal Albert Hall for a day of Bible teaching and praise to God. As a result, we now have a Men's breakfast once a month at church.

R is for Romania. We visited some friends who were with us for several years at Borthwick Free. Their church is the largest Baptist church in Europe and we once again proved that in a place of material poverty the Lord has chosen to bless in a remarkable way, with true riches.

X is for Xtension! We are delighted with our additional space at church, though it is filling up and we have already had some full houses. Praise the Lord!

Well, we hope you haven't become like zombies as you have trawled through the twenty-six letters above. We want to leave you with our love for a blessed Christmas and our hope that you are trusting in The Alpha and Omega, The Beginning and The End, The Eternal One. He is Emmanuel, God with us! Much love...

Sometimes, though, the Lord's help comes on a more mundane level.

Now, *with my computer resurrected through Jesus's provision of parts, and the help of friends in our Christian Fellowship...*

WE *are waiting for God to tell Trevor what his next job ought to be.*

I wonder what God will say? 'Supply teachers are always in demand, but there's probably more money in plumbing these days.'

But there is no denying that while religion brings peace and happiness to many, to some it brings only chagrin.

DAD *keeps well and in remarkably good health. The further loss of his sight and the impairment of his short-term memory have aged him — but he is still remarkable for ninety-eight. He enjoys going to the Methodist church every Sunday although he gets very upset that the minister doesn't wear the clerical collar.*

The recipient has scrawled crossly in the margin, 'Blind man upset by "inappropriate" dress code!'

Some people just don't get on with others of the same faith. This is from Lancashire:

AFTER *an unsettled period of discontent, we finally left our church after more than ten years. We had been unhappy at the change of vicar, and in particular his bullish and arrogant leadership style and lack of emotional intelligence. We gave him one last chance at the annual meeting in April but the whole thing was a charade which failed to see the mass exodus of faithful worshippers as anything other than 'chaff'.*

Another writer does not waste time taking issue with mere vicars:

I AM *of the firm conviction that Christmas is a festival, which should be enjoyed and celebrated by all mankind, which leads me on to a thought. 'What if Jesus Christ were to reappear in our midst today?' One thing is for sure. He would do a double-take upon*

> *our modern day Esau, none other than the new Archbishop of*
> *Canterbury, Dr Rowan Williams, who has carefully cultivated*
> *an unkempt and dishevelled appearance, which is frightening*
> *to behold, and in defiance of the law of Leviticus, wherein it is*
> *required that all priests be without physical blemish.*

Like so many modern round robins, this letter includes a footnote, explaining that the reference to Esau is from the bible: 'for my brother Esau is an hairy man…'

Recent events have caused problems especially for Americans, who tend to bombard their British friends with Christian explanations of, say, the attack on the World Trade Center.

> I AM *often asked what God was doing on 9 / 1 1. Why was He not*
> *protecting and caring for His people? Well, I can tell you what He*
> *was doing. He was organising traffic jams near Logan airport,*
> *Boston, so that there would be fewer people on the flights that were*
> *hijacked. At the same time He was arranging for more heavy traffic*
> *in the lower Manhattan area, so that many people would not arrive*
> *on time for their work in the Twin Towers. In short, He was doing all*
> *he could…*

This notion of God as the Fourth Emergency Service seems to be on fairly shaky doctrinal ground. It appears to deny His omnipotence, as well as being rather hurtful for relatives and friends of those who set off early enough to reach the airport or the World Trade Center. Still, no doubt many of those who did lose loved ones will have sent Christmas letters in 2001 explaining how their faith sustained them through the intolerable grief...

A Suffolk reader – a retired vicar himself – writes that he married an American woman in the 1950s and spent many years in the US before retiring home in Britain. 'We therefore receive vast quantities of circular Christmas letters, most of which throw us into quagmires of desperation. Here are a couple of the best from this year's batch':

> THIS *year Moma is spending Christmas with Jesus, looking down on the lights and Christmas trees of Florida, and smiling her lovely smile on all of us.*

> WE *thank the Lord that he has blessed America with the gift of President George Bush, a profoundly God-fearing Christian man of great spiritual depth and high intellectual leadership.* [in the margin] *You folks in merry old England must be so grateful to have Mr Blare* [sic] *as your wonderful prime minister.*

One is reminded of those footballers who pray that God will help their team to win. But then it is startling how many round robinners simply assume that others share their faith:

> I HOPE *that, however hectic your Christmas festivities, you will find room for the Christ Child.*

Another family went on a tour of the Far East and marvelled at:

THE WAY *God kept us safe both in all our travelling and in our health, and the real sense of His hand was upon us in all our journey.*

This came in the same month as one of those terrible Filipino ferry disasters in which almost a hundred people died. Evidently God was too busy shielding a visiting English couple to pay heed to them.

Oh Dear, What a Plonker!

'I HATE THESE people, hate them, hate them, hate them!' That's a fairly typical reaction to many of the circular letters that wing my way. 'I was appalled by their effusions, as always,' says one recipient, who has, in a fury, gone through the entire letter, which is only one typed sheet of A4 paper, and found no fewer than twenty-seven grammatical and punctuation errors and marked them in a black, angry pen.

It is quite startling how loathed many of the letters are. In some cases it's the smugness, the failure to recognize that other people's lives might be more difficult and more complicated than the bland and prosperous existence enjoyed by the writers. Often it's the blithe assumption that the recipients have both the time and the inclination to plough through thousands of words describing every tiny detail of of someone else's life. When, as is often the case, the recipient hasn't set eyes on the round robinner for many years, the anger mounts to dangerous levels. Some people evidently think that the letters have some evil power that can harm their lives.

I WAS *going to throw this away, but I thought that my waste-paper basket was too good for it. Instead I am sending it to you. You cannot believe the relief I will feel when it is out of my house.*

> WE GET *these every year from somebody I was at university with thirty years ago. They are all exactly the same — one and a half pages of excruciating detail about his job and financial situation (including lots of back-biting about ex- or existing colleagues, followed by a cursory paragraph or two about his family).*

Some writers clearly regard the letter as just one of the many ways to inflict their own lives on people who are virtual strangers:

> WE SEE *this man only once a year, and we don't know any of his family except his wife. He did, however, entertain us for over an hour at a dinner party with his map and photos, on his laptop, and commentary on their Indian trip. His newsletters generally end up in the bin, unread.*

Often people read letters to the end in spite of themselves.

> THE ENCLOSED *is from a friend I knew at university, but whom I have seen only once in the last thirty-seven years. I have never met any of the eleven people he refers to. I confess I felt guilty afterwards about having laughed uproariously about the old lady with one leg 'who we advised to get a ground-floor apartment', and I loved the ending, 'well, you've had your page', presumably reflecting the enormous demand from the Hunters' friends for this offering, which Jim has had to be coerced into satisfying!*

But round robinners are rarely deterred by not knowing their recipients:

THE extraordinary thing is that we scarcely know the people who have sent it. They lived down the road from us for a couple of years. And we know none of the other people mentioned... but what a bugger those two days of constipation must have been!

I CAN'T resist sending this – it's from a cousin who I have seen once in fifty-five years!

PLEASE find enclosed a Christmas letter from a friend from the past I haven't seen for at least twenty-two years. The people she mentions I have never heard of, let alone met. Jerry, who she talks about, is her son, whom she left with her husband when he was three years old, and Pat and Di are her present husband's children whom he left when they were children. She writes about them as though either of them had anything to do with their bringing up.

THIS woman was a subordinate of mine in a laboratory about twenty years ago. I have seen her probably only once since them. I may not ever have seen her children at all, let alone her friends or dogs... It is an annual saga of a middle-aged Miss Piggy and her accountant husband, their cloned children and their stunningly ordinary existence. Are they blinkered and arrogant, or naïve to the point of gormlessness, or so aspiring upper middle-class as to become ridiculous? I suspect they are completely unaware of other people's sensitivities.

I USED *to work with this man in Croydon. I expect I never made it plain enough that we didn't want this sort of tosh because it is, in a Pooterish way, often quite hilarious. This year we got two. I believe that qualifies as cruel and unusual punishment.*

I HAVE *never met these people, and my wife's name is not Sue!*

Some senders are clearly oblivious to the rage they inspire in the recipients:

THOSE WHO *insist on disseminating such gruesome nonsense deserve to be publicly shamed, so I regret your assurance of anonymity. Our only relationship with the perpetrator of this self-important rubbish is that we bought a business from her and the John referred to in the last paragraph (they were then what these days passes for a happily married couple) and they ripped us off something rotten. She seems to think that we ought to retain an everlasting interest in her and her gruesome children. How can anyone produce such drivel and not see that the sole reaction of any sane recipient must be a good, paragraph by paragraph, belly laugh?*

THIS WHOLE *thing is a classic of its kind. The smug, self-satisfied tone and the false modesty are maintained throughout... the meeting with 'Sir' Mick Jagger ('we ended up having dinner with him — as you do') and being stupidly busy, constantly disorganized, tumbling on from month to month. Gosh!*

THIS MAN *is my oldest and dearest friend, but, oh dear, what a plonker!*

THESE PEOPLE *give it to us with both barrels. Roger is boastful, and his wife Caroline is devastatingly crass.*

THE AMAZING *thing about this letter is that we have never met the writer. Her partner is no more than an acquaintance, whom we knew about ten years ago when his children went to the same school as ours, while he was in another marriage. Help — I'm starting to produce a circular here myself!*

THE ENCLOSED *letter was sent to my stepmother. Nobody in the family knows who George and Babs are, and my father, Albert, to whom it is also addressed, died two years ago. We therefore have not the remotest interest in this couple. I'm ashamed to say that our hearts sank when we got to the end and discovered that George and Babs are quite well.*

THIS LETTER *actually comes to the family from whom we bought our house, ten years ago. The people who sent it obviously haven't taken the hint of no reply for a decade.*

AN ACQUAINTANCE *of mine, I will call her M, has been sending out self-centred circular letters for some years. They consist solely of a detailed catalogue of her many foreign holidays, about which she manages to tell us everything that is not interesting and to miss out all the many things about the country she is visiting that one might be curious about... I enclose this for your enjoyment, and in the hope that you will dispose of it as safely as possible. I thought you might share my joy at reading that 'the new photos start in volume 4, page 6'. Oh, goody!*

It was certainly hard to get beyond the first paragraph of that particular letter, which picked up from an earlier communication describing M's holiday in Latin America. She leaves her underwear to dry by the hotel pool, and forgets to pick it up when she checks out later in the day:

I GOT through to the hotel on the phone, but to no avail. When I returned no one would admit to any knowledge of the call, and the owner reminded me that they were not responsible. This then resulted in complicated arrangements to get a replacement bra bought for me in England and posted over to the US. You can't easily buy sized bras in Latin America.

And did Bruce Chatwin die in vain?

Now and again, for reasons of the purest malice, recipients like to get letters or at least regret missing some. Jude Evans writes from Bridgwater:

PERHAPS the most interesting circular letter will be one I never received. A school friend of my daughter failed to get the 3 As at A-level which were predicted. Distraught, she turned to her parents for comfort. The mother's response? She wailed, 'Oh, no! What on

earth will we say now in the Christmas family newsletter?' You can
imagine what the previous years' letters were like.

If the writers realized the effect they were having on people they
at least think of as friends, or close acquaintances, they would
surely never write again.

It is puzzling why people send such infuriating letters. Are they
simply lacking in any degree of self-awareness? Is it a socially
acceptable form of boasting and status-seeking? After all, nobody
would phone someone they had met once in twenty years purely
to brag that they were off on a Caribbean cruise, or that their son
had got three As. You'd be astonished if you got a postcard in June
informing you that the husband of a woman your wife met at a
conference in 1987 had just bought himself a new Porsche with
fuel injection and twin carbs. Yet circular leters do exactly that.

WHAT *drives us into a rage is the crassness and sheer idleness of*
the senders, so obviously using the same word-processor template
year after year. Same typography, same paragraph structure, the
intro and grinning mugshots, the list of Nigel's latest small-press
non-books, Rachel's dull IT career, their bloody annual Greek
holiday, and the news, with solemn circular vignette, of the latest
relative to 'pass away' (though at least this year we weren't asked
to sign the memorial guestbook on the Internet).

For some people, the letters bring more than just a niggling
annoyance.

> THIS *round robin letter from a cousin and her husband (who I haven't seen in years, and am unlikely to in the future) does not just make me sigh with boredom at the banality of its contents, but lights up a small furnace of irritation and anger that they should think that I would be in any degree interested in her life, her family, and of course her numerous grandchildren. My cousin was constantly held up as the model daughter — so accomplished and so successful. And, as you can see, she has gone on to produce these wonderkids, plus a plethora of grandchildren. (I have only one.) As you can see, this well-meant missile that comes winging its way can have a devastating effect, reminding one of past failures and unrealized dreams. It brings up in me lashings of self-pity.*

Some writers seem to imagine that the wretched recipients memorize the letters from year to year, regarding each one as the latest instalment in some gripping serial. Others offer to fill in the gaps.

> IMPOSSIBLE *to believe that Christmas is upon us again. For 2003 please re-read the letter for 2002 as we have continued in much the same vein (available on request).*

> THOSE *of you who followed our story through to the end of last year will remember . . .*

One new menace is the Internet. Some writers offer further information on their Internet site, as if the 3,000 words they have already sent is the merest taste of the delights that recipients could enjoy. Others – and this is a growing threat – actually include the appropriate web address for everything they have done, so you don't just have to read about their holiday in Corfu, but can actually flesh out the details with the Corfu tourist board site so you can learn even more about the Brothertons' holiday! To say nothing of their children's schools sites, from which you can download pictures of their offspring as third shepherd, or the writer's employer's site, or even the site for the new car he bought and describes in quite painful detail later in the letter.

So how do the recipients of these ghastly missives cope? In many different ways. Some send them on with enraged comments in the margin: 'Ha, bloody ha!' at some choice misfortune. 'This is the bit that made me fling the whole thing away with a shout of rage and anguish!' One woman tore the whole thing up into tiny pieces, then realized it would be better therapy to send the letter in. She must have spent a long time sellotaping it back together. One technique popular these days is to send spoof letters to the original perpetrators:

> IN *summer Teddy managed a successful single-handed expedition to the summit of Mount Everest, returning home to find that Darren's new album had just hit number one in the charts. We have had less luck with Debbie, but her probation officer assures us she should be back on the straight and narrow soon!*

SIMON HOGGART

'I don't know any of these people, why on earth should I care about their holiday plans?' says one recipient. A writer describes how her new dog is perfect in almost every way, adding: 'His only fault is barking at cars. He is having a healer do something about it.' The reader's comment in the margin is 'I nearly pulled a stomach muscle.' One writer makes the mistake — having described at length his own gorgeous property in Provence — of adding: 'I hope we can visit your own lovely home again some day.' 'Not bloody likely, if this is what we have to put up with!' the aggrieved recipient has scrawled at the bottom.

Another recipient got it off her chest by providing a commentary almost as long as the letter itself. She quotes from it, with her own footnotes, like the concordance to a Shakespeare play:

'I WALKED *the Pennine Way with help from my chauffeuse over several days and weekends, and Tim, Tricia and Malcolm who helped out with transport, and D, B&B between the M62 and Ponden Reservoir.'* Who [the recipient asks] *are T, T, M, D, B&B?' to say nothing of Ponden Reservoir. 'Chauffeuse' is Nick's typical pomposity, and refers to his wife Kate having to do all the donkey work.*

So great is the writer's anger that she hasn't spotted that D, B&B aren't people at all, but stand for dinner, bed and breakfast.

In the same way, others summarise the letters as a means of getting the fury out of their system.

THIS *letter gets longer every year. It's much worse now that some of the children, all brilliant it goes without saying, have grown up and have boyfriends — we are subjected to added news not only about the boyfriends who we have never met, but even about the BOYFRIENDS' PARENTS!!! The formula is:*

1. *Husband is utterly brilliant from every point of view.*
2. *Ditto the wife.*
3. *Both sing brilliantly and we hear an account of all the productions they have sung in.*
4. *Eldest daughter brilliant.*
5. *Ditto next daughter.*
6. *Ditto the son who has moved on from being brilliant with his toys to being a brilliant photographer...*
9. *News of the superb Christmas they are about to have, and news of respective mothers who are, it goes without saying, totally wonderful even though frail.*

You just know that the poor recipient felt far, far better after she had written all that. One reader points out:

AN INTERESTING *question is WHY don't people have an in-built filter system — as in, 'How does this read? Will it be of any interest to anyone?'*

This reader has spotted the penultimate sentence: 'Our diary is full for the coming festive season, with dinner parties, and concerts, and receptions, etc. etc.' and marked it: 'Pass the sick bucket'.

Sometimes people get their revenge by writing the truth about people's lives in their covering notes:

> AN ADDED irony about this self-praising rubbish is that both him and her are well known for their affairs and casual screwing, so the stories about their happy, settled life are all the more pointless to those receiving them.

Others, perhaps aware of the distress caused by circular letters, have gone the opposite route. One six-line letter lists various minor vexations in the senders' lives.

> As WE didn't find them all that interesting ourselves, we don't really think you would either. So you wouldn't miss anything by being told all the details. But all the best for the New Year.

Another says at the top, 'Christmas newsletter, December 2003', and at the bottom, 'All the best, Dave'. The rest of the sheet contains only the words: 'This page intentionally left blank'.

The Whole Darn Human Race

SOME ROUND ROBINNERS think it's a good idea to make their letter stand out from the pack, and they've tried several ways of doing it. Most of these prove to be mistakes. Take the notion of writing up your year in verse. You are not TS Eliot, Andrew Motion, or even Pam Ayres. What you will probably produce is, sadly, not poetry but doggerel. Take this letter from Kent, consisting of forty-four stanzas of a consistent standard, which you can judge:

> BEFORE *we move on to the tribe,*
> *Our holiday we must describe.*
> *We went back to Greece,*
> *Tranquillity and peace*
> *With plenty of wine to imbibe.*
>
> *For once we were all on our own*
> *The photographs need to be shown*
> *We had a great time*
> *The sea was sublime*
> *With new friends, so never alone.*

The last stanza implies what literary critics call a type of ambiguity, in that they were all on their own, and yet never alone. This is either an example of higher metaphysics, or else the writer was short of a rhyme. They go for a speedboat ride:

THE DRIVER *was grinning with fun*
His passengers be spilled, and undone
By shifting his weight
The anchor his fate
Kevin's bulk seemed more than a ton.

One son has gone into the law, and here the language becomes spare, even elliptical:

ON FRANCIS *it's now time to focus*
But the law seems to be all hocus pocus
Fifty words used,
All are confused
The language was not meant to choke us.

'Tis a conversion course that he's taking
And the second year that he's making
Next year he'll work,
No time to shirk
But the money he soon will be raking.

This family in the south adopt the same basic form. They have just stopped working:

So now John's retired
His hobbies can start.
One day he'll be playing
A saxophone part.

He still has his fingers
In several pies;
Sits on two committees
And keeps local ties.

You sometimes wish correspondents would try to write real poetry; at least you'd feel they'd put some effort into it: 'April was the cruellest month / But Kitty – green fingers! – managed to breed lilacs out of the dead land. She also mixed memory and desire on the Aga and raised £27 for the church steeple fund by selling the result! Well done, her!'

This is from a well-travelled family who manage to encapsulate each trip in a few terse lines:

2003 was a very good year
For Withrows and family alike
We travelled again to places like Spain
But not on a motorbike.

In February our van took us just locally
But England still has its charm

In a Lakeland village we stayed for a while
And rested, safe from harm.

For Sally's big five-oh
We went to a town renowned for art and leisure
We stayed for a while under Florence's spell
And of culture we had a large measure.

Lloyd finally got his reward for hard work
With an MBA degree
Conferred on him at a ceremony
At Southampton University.

This is from America:

THEN, *followed by Chuck Reiss's Volkswagen bus,*
We brought Aunt Ruth back for a visit with us.

Some people seem to feel that poesy is one way they can improve
the lot of mankind. This is from a British couple who now live in
the US:

BETH *and I went off a-cruisin'*
Lots of eats, a little boozin'
We steamed from California's sunny shore.
Catalonia was delightful,
Mexicanos were politeful.

Soon 'twill be two-ought-ought-two,

There's so much we want to do,

To make the New Year count in every way.

Let us make a better place,

For the whole darn human race.

This next 'poem' is rather unnerving, in that it is devoted entirely
to the subject of why the writers are sending it in the first place:

WE have a list of folks we know, all written in a book

And every year when Christmas comes, we go and take a look.

And that is when we realize that these names are a part

Not of the book they're written in, but of our very heart.

For each name stands for someone who has crossed our path some time

And in that meeting they've become the rhythm in each rhyme,

And while it sounds fantastic for us to make this claim

We really feel that we're composed of each remembered name.

And while you may not be aware of any 'special link'

Just meeting you has changed our life a lot more than you think.

For once we've met somebody, the years cannot erase

The memory of a pleasant word or of a friendly face.

For we are but the total of the many folks we've met

And you happen to be one of those we prefer not to forget

And whether we have known you for many years or few

In some way you have had a part in shaping things we do.

You realise, as this unspools for several more verses, that it might be going out to people they met once at a party, or who possibly told them where to find the bus stop. Now they are doomed to receive a missive like this, every year of their lives...

Another well-loved technique among circular-writers is to produce a letter as if written by your pet. This may sound charming, but it creates a problem. Either you keep the whole thing in character, so to speak, concentrating on circumstances and events which a pet might find interesting if it could write, or even think very much, or else you have the pet describe the family's year – in which case it quickly becomes painfully anthropomorphic. This letter swerves giddily between the two. It's from a dog called Micky, who lives with an English family in Spain:

> JIM *looked me in the eye, which usually means bad stuff. 'Why don't you write the Christmas letter, Micky?' OK, I will. First, I want to say something about cats. If you've got a problem with cats, e-mail me. I'll be right over. Second, on the subject of fish-hooks, don't eat them, even if they are wrapped up in sardines!*

So far, in the great tradition of *Animal Farm*, *Watership Down*, *Black Beauty* and so forth. But then we leave doggy topics and move on to a lengthy list of visitors from the UK, local politics, the problems of acquiring residency rights and planning permission – subjects that, frankly, would not greatly concern most dogs. But it ends:

Jim *says, 'That's enough! Say "Merry Christmas and Happy New Year"'. OK. And remember what I told you, good grub at the skips!*

A family in the north-west have another new wrinkle. Part of their letter is evidently written by their two dogs, as if to another dog in the neighbourhood.

Hi, *Smudger! Can we introduce ourselves? We are the Moorbank House dogs — we live just across the churchyard from you. I'm HIS dog and my name is Arthur — I'm a black Labrador and my assistant dog is HER dog and called Pansy... of course we're not allowed out of our garden unsupervised so can't visit you in yours — the pond sounds rather fun. However, if one of THEIR visitors leaves a front door open, the temptation for me to go for a walk and visit the Co-op rubbish bags is too great — I'm never popular when I return.*

Our cats, Sydney (who is the same colour as me and my best friend) and Emily get into trouble over feathered things too. Emily thinks she can get round us by putting presents of field mice and voles on our bed, but we don't really like them — too crunchy.

Inevitably the segment is signed with a winsome paw print...

Here's a dog that apparently believes in too much sharing as well:

I say *it's been a peaceful year, but that's a bit of a lie. I had two dreadful bouts of worms in April and in October. Worms are something I would not wish on my worst enemy — well, perhaps, just on Mugs, that sex-obsessed dog up the road.*

This letter starts in canine style:

Hi, *Folks, You may have seen me in that advert where I run around with the Andrex toilet paper, but you didn't know my name — HAMISH… now I have Stripes and the other cats under my control, and I have Derek and June wrapped around my paw! Actually, the only word I can read is 'puppy'. If they try to give me food with that on the label I won't touch it! I'd rather have old dead rabbit, rotting mice or Weetabix — they are really good.*

Delightful though this is, it could get a little wearing. So poor Hamish is soon reduced to bringing us tidings of the household humans.

On *Friday morning, Tim and Grace were in a car accident and not well enough to travel from Winchester. Alhamdulilah! They are all right but both had whiplash injuries, which take time to go away… 19th July was a wonderful day when Neil and Helena were married. Most of the family were there but not everyone could make it. D & J enjoyed seeing Neil's godfathers, Jack and Sean, together again. Neil has left the licensed trade, he says, for more settled hours…*

We seem to have strayed some way from the dog bowl, filled as it is with rotting mice and Weetabix. But the news must out:

—

D & J *are still playing bridge, golf and tennis. Derek is secretary of the local show and Grace is chairman of the church restoration project. They are never bored!*

Unlike some of their readers, one fears.

One family from East Anglia, from their letter of distinctly mystic bent, wrote their annual letter for years as if from their dog Webster. However, at some point in 2003 this much-loved animal companion (a Labrador, according to the drawing of him sporting wings and a halo) passed away. But such a minor development would not stop any determined round robinner, and their latest letter is headlined 'Hello From Heaven'.

IT *probably won't come as a huge surprise when I tell you that these greetings come to you from my new home in the Happy Hunting Ground. I have to say that I'm immensely relieved to have moved on at last, and shaken off the shackles of earthly life. As my old mistress used to say, 'old age is NO FUN', and like her I found the prospect of discovering Nirvana 'wildly exciting'. And I can assure you: it is Heavenly! Pastures New are very much to my liking... now my body lies four foot down, deep in the underworld in one of my favourite places in the garden, with Michaelmas daisies and lilies on top and a shark's fin headstone to speed my night sea-crossing...*

Happily, before leaving for 'The Great Awakening', Webster managed to scratch out some family news.

WELL, *Bridget returned from India as Balambika (having been initiated into yogic practices), cleared the sitting room and turned it into an ashram, only to abandon us all again in search of further enlightenment, this time in Thailand with her friend James. Her first e-mails described in detail their bowel movements during an eight-day fasting cleanse...*

It is commonplace for families to give space to every member, from the oldest to the youngest, to describe their year. This next letter, however, seems to be unique in being written by a five-month-old foetus, already named Ben:

WELL, *you haven't met me before. It's a bit dark in here, but nice and warm. The only complaint is that I don't have much choice for the menu, but I'll change all that in a few months' time. I'm starting to make my presence felt by giving Martha a kick or two. I'll be leaving my present accommodation around mid-April...*

One of the saddest letters comes in the form of a crossword. At first it looks quite jolly, with a smiling snowman and sprigs of holly decorating the top. But it conceals a tragic secret. It was clearly a dreadful year for these people, which you can follow by reading the clues and then the answers:

1. DOWN, *'An insult after years of hard work' (JOB SEEKERS' ALLOWANCE); 2. Down, 'What we often felt' (FED UP); 8. Across, 'Frightening road to freedom' (REDUNDANCY); 16. Across,*

'Cheap holiday' (CAMPING); and 9. Across: 'Units consumed increased' (ALCOHOL)

But of course it ends with 20. Down, 'What we wish you all!' (MERRY CHRISTMAS). For in the world of round robins, being dejected is the ultimate loss of face.

Dining Table for Sale. Any Offers?

IT IS INEVITABLE that the Grim Reaper must visit many round robinners every year. But of course he is rarely ushered in by the front door. Instead he tends to be sent round to the tradesman's entrance, tucked away towards the back of the letter, not permitted to spoil the permanent hectic celebrations in the living room.

> SADLY, *Richard's mother died after a long illness while Richard was in Hong Kong. He could not interrupt the trip, so was unable to attend her funeral. But I feel that the rest of the family gave her a fitting send-off.*

Frankly, you suspect from reading some of the letters, more old people ought to do the decent thing and expire after a reasonable time.

> ROGER'S *mother died on the 22nd, though it was really a relief as she had been confined to bed for so long.*

These people want to give a loved one a fitting memorial, and how better than by spending money on themselves?

> MOTHER *died just before we were about to go on holiday to the*

Seychelles. We decided to go ahead anyway, but next year we plan
a visit to California in her memory.

You sometimes wonder how hurt some folk would be if they knew how their shuffling off this mortal coil was shuffled off in turn by their nearest and dearest.

TRAGEDY *struck in August with the unexpected death of Jane's*
brother Colin. My absence drifting across the Irish Sea in a
becalmed race was not helpful. This was exacerbated by a foul
return sail from Plymouth with a crew of four, two being seasick
and a 20-knot wind on the nose, all the way home. Anyway I had
my best ever result, coming 23rd out of fifty-seven in Class 1.

In spite of this, Colin did not die in vain. He furnished a useful lesson for life:

HE *had sufficient savings to have done many more things than he*
ever did. So, folks, go out and spend! Your children certainly won't
need it, or ever thank you for leaving it to them in your will!

One letter does at least begin with fourteen lines detailing how the writer's mother died – followed by eleven lines on the passing of their cat. Luckily the family bounces back:

OUR *summer holiday plans were obviously affected by mum's death,*
but in July we were able to get a last-minute booking for a week in a
villa in Corfu. The villa was lovely, the weather perfect, and we had

> *no disasters… this part of the island is very* Sunday Times —
> *apologies to the* Guardian, *but the image isn't quite the same!*

It's amazing how a trip can perk people up, even after multiple bereavements:

> DURING *this period we lost Sandy, our gardener for thirty-six years (he came with the house) at the age of eighty-three; an ex-colleague from my firm who died of CJD; and a very longstanding friend, Tom Rogers, who died from cancer of the pancreas and liver. By way of compensation we took a day trip to France by Eurotunnel — very cheap at £9 return.*

Some parents, however, merit only one line:

> IN APRIL *Jim, Jamie's father, died after a short illness — he was seventy-eight.*

This parent doesn't even appear to have a name:

> JUST *last month, Molly's mother died. Her good humour was not diminished by the development of Alzheimers. She will be missed by all.*

This sad single lines come after a lengthy description of an infestation which damaged the Brussels sprouts in the garden:

> SADLY, *both our new neighbours died within six months of each other.*

Many parents lose any sense of timing when it comes to joining the Choir Invisible:

> MONDAY 30th December was scheduled for our New Year family gathering, this time with Shauna and Graham, plus Nicky, Helen, Martin, Trevor and Charles. In the morning the nursing home telephoned to say that Mum had had a fall. Peter went to visit, collecting Shauna en route. Mum seemed comfortable but sleepy, and after a while the pair returned so that Peter could dispense pre-dinner drinks and then carve the largest piece of beef that we had had for years. However, before the carving knife could even be sharpened, the nursing home phoned again to say that Mum had taken a turn for the worse. Peter and Martin rushed there, but too late. She died at 1.20, shortly before they arrived. We became a melancholy gathering, augmented by Pam and Andrew, with no appetite for a house full of food.

What a waste!

In spite of this, old people can have their uses, if only for recycling all that food:

> TIM'S time is taken up at the moment organizing the bridge club and seeing to the needs of his Mum, who unfortunately seems to have gone downhill fairly rapidly over the last couple of months. However, on Janice's soups, consisting of our leftovers liquidized, she seems to be picking up a little.

Other mums, however, die in a fine fashion. As you read this you feel the theme music from *Gone with the Wind* should strike up:

> MOM *died a few weeks ago. It was an intensely beautiful time,*
> *waiting with her as she died, in her own room in Charleston, in*
> *the bed I'd crept into when I felt restless as a child... her breathing*
> *was so laboured, struggling to get air through the fluid that filled*
> *her body. Her kidneys had shut down. Now the toxins had nowhere*
> *to go... Mom hung on as hour after hour passed. I met with*
> *the household staff... I told them they could say goodbye. A*
> *housekeeper held her hand, brown clasping beige, thanking her*
> *for treating her 'with equality'. For her last hour, Mom's bed was*
> *piled high with children and grandchildren, singing one Southern*
> *Baptist hymn after another and show tunes from* Oklahoma.

Surely they weren't encouraging the old lady to go?

There's a famous story about the Scotsman who puts an ad in the Births, Marriages and Deaths section: 'McTavish dead'. The clerk at the paper explains that he can have five words for the minimum charge, so he changes the ad to: 'McTavish dead. Fiesta for sale.' I was reminded of the gag by this letter:

> AFTER *a long illness, which she bore with little complaint, my*
> *Mum died in November. We are now the owners of a fine drop-leaf*
> *dining table. Any offers?*

Payment in Canned Goose Liver

THE GREATEST PITFALL of all in circular letters is smugness. It is a trap that only a few writers trouble to avoid. You half expect them to begin: 'Well, it's been another record smug year for the Yarborough family, with smug levels at an all-time high! Everything we have done makes us feel better about ourselves, our achievements and our good fortune, while probably making you feel like an inadequate worm!'

For some reason, Australians can be among the worst offenders:

> EACH time we return from overseas we are reminded just how much we are all very blessed to be living in this paradise called Australia. Long may it continue.

They like to rub it in.

These people were distressed by England's victory over Australia in the rugby world cup final in 2003, though evidently not for long:

> TO the English relos, we thought we had better let you win something. We're happy with the cricket, tennis, soccer, swimming, hockey, rugby league and the weather.

They beat us at hockey too? And we're supposed to care?

This is from a British couple who visited Australia:

IT's *amazing how long it takes to get through customs at Sydney airport when the customs officials ask your wife to remove her jewellery, which is a bit difficult when she's got more jewellery on worth more than the gross domestic product of some small Third World country. And she couldn't get it all off! Eventually one of the feds used one of those metallic scanner things and they let her through – which was a bit of a bugger, because the holiday ended up costing me three times what it would have cost if they'd arrested her.*

But complacency can be found everywhere. Here's a woman who uses her failure to ski as the opportunity for a sidelong boast:

AT *the New Year, the four of us went skiing for the first time. I thought that I would probably be okay at skiing, being sort of fit and sort of adventurous. But I found out that I was a skiing wimp, a coward, altogether pressure-on-the-front-footily challenged! However, Natasha and Jack assured me that it was okay, they still loved me. 'You don't have to be good at everything, Mummy!'*

Sometimes people's wonderful lives can get just a touch annoying. This family live in rural Yorkshire:

AS *we write our annual Christmas letter, it is a glorious sunny, crisp morning as we look out over the fields from an upper room and realize we have been at Thornthwaite for five years. We have been so lucky to have found a place that gives us such joy and the*

*opportunity for realizing our creative skills, as well as receiving
visitors from far and wide who marvel at the peace and tranquillity
of our home and its surrounding countryside.*

They install an irrigation system from a never-ending spring:

As *the heat of June, July and August bore down on the gardens of
our village, the irrigation system at Thornthwaite paid huge
dividends as the sprinkler systems squirted into action each
evening, both in the flower garden at the back and the kitchen
garden. Much joy and satisfaction was experienced as we gathered
our garden produce throughout the summer and enjoyed the marvel
of flowers planted as seedlings bursting into bloom.*

You find yourself wanting to yell, 'but it's so much simpler to go
to Tesco!'

TED *fulfilled a long-held ambition by going to hear the whole
Ring Cycle in Budapest, with subtitles in Hungarian. His Inuit
book is coming out in Hungarian translation in January, with
royalties paid in canned goose liver.*

Mmm. Make a note to pop round and visit them at dinner time!

But the future of the round-robin letter is clearly on the
Internet. Why bother printing it all up and paying postage when
people can access every detail of your lives by hitting a few keys?
A reader sent in a ten-page letter that begins:

WE'VE *been debating the future of our letters. We've had many nice compliments on our epistles, and no one has been rude about them. Now and again Dan receives e-mail out of the blue from strangers who discover the letters* <u>on the Web</u> *— recently we had fan mail complimenting us on our fifteen-year-old description of* germknödel, *an amazing Austrian dessert! So, here we go again, with a firm resolve to curb the pen and make this letter shorter. The year, like others, seems to have brought the usual amalgam of family (eventful), music (eclectic), sailing (exciting), travel (exotic), teaching (effective, we hope) and research (erudite) — with some farmyard adventures thrown in. Are we getting in a rut?*

Dear me, no. And in case you want to read even more about these people, their letter ends with good news:

OUR *millennium project is to produce a compendium of Christmas letters, dating back to when we started in 1985. We're raiding the family photograph album to get a colour picture for each page. But don't worry: you won't get a copy — there are 150 pages and we can't afford such a large printing. But you will be able to download it from the Net. Watch this space!*

Finally, one of the best ways of coping with round robin letters was sent by Alison Davies of Hanworth, Middlesex. As a child she played a game called Winkle's Wedding, in which the narrative was interrupted by gaps in the text. These had to be filled in by the players shouting out random words from a set of cards that had been dealt out to them.

ENTER *the spectre of the Christmas newsletter. One day, while reading yet another missive of fact-laden, self-congratulatory prose, which had fallen smugly from a Christmas card, it suddenly dawned on me that I held in my hand the perfect updated raw material for a reinvigorated version of the game which had thrilled me as a child.*

A few minutes' effort spent writing a list of common, or not so common, nouns on small sheets of paper — a brief glance at this year's shows 'piano-shaped swimming pool', 'truss', 'soggy tissue' — is followed by a businesslike reading out loud of any of these letters, leaving a pause at the right moment. (Try lists of academic achievements, or stories of home improvements.) One of the other players reads out the next word on his or her list. No choice can be allowed; it must be the next noun. In this fashion we have received the news that one correspondent was 'knocked over by an over-friendly CHICKEN McNUGGET', and another's child 'has joined THE THIRD REICH which does excellent work in church and youth clubs'.

The Hamster that Loved Puccini
—

The Peccadillo of Proud Parenthood

OF ALL THE SINS committed by the senders of Christmas newsletters, an excessive admiration for their offspring is probably the worst – certainly the one most likely to drive recipients into a demented rage. What is it with these children, with their perfect exam results, their thespian abilities, sporting talent, musical genius and part-time charity work? Don't they ever get drunk at a friend's house, watch too much television, smoke pot or even answer back? Do none of them wear hoodies, or swear, or eat junk food instead of tofu sandwiches? I suspect what makes these children so infuriating is the knowledge that most of them probably do some of those things; it's just that their parents have decided to ignore such topics for the purpose of the Christmas letter. And, since we can presume that most of the children see the letters, the writers see it as an easy way to earn parental brownie points – 'of course she knows how much we admire what she does; we put it in this year's letter, didn't we?'

None of this can be much consolation to those who receive the bulletins.

MY EARS *ringing with praise of Jake from his teachers at our termly parent–teacher evening, I got home to find Emily opening a*

letter telling her that she had won a place at Oxford! To read
medicine, no less! Gordon Brown, eat your heart out. It is a four-
year course, so she has had to postpone her gap year in Latin
America.

To which the only possible response is 'Oh no, must you do this
to us?'

CHLOE *wins the prize for most activities. In music, she continues*
with the recorders, violin and piano and has now taken up the flute
as well. She is in the Junior School orchestra and wind band.
Recently she had an audition for the national preparation schools
orchestra, was selected for the orchestra itself (violin) and so will
spend a week in Norfolk next summer. She also won cups at school
for the best string player, and as a member of the top ensemble.
After-school activities include netball, gymnastics, tap, ballet,
tennis and Girl Guides. In swimming she won a gold medal at the
county age group championships as a member of the relay team and
has represented her club and school in many galas. She also has had
one of her works of art mounted in the entrance foyer of the school.
As a postscript, school work seems to be progressing without
noticeable effort.

You have to feel sorry for her younger brother, Ifan, who is 'altogether more laid back... he very much enjoys relaxing at home,
goes to bed late and gets up late...' Suspicions grow in the

reader's mind. Is Ifan not an achiever like his big sister? Not an achiever? Are you mad?

> *Earlier this year Ifan played from memory the slow movement of the Rachmaninov piano concerto no. 2 at a school concert, and later won the Junior Mozart Cup at our city music festival. He will play bassoon for the under-21 wind band, and will go on a concert tour this summer in Paris and the Loire Valley. He very much enjoys tennis, swimming, hockey and also plays bridge for the school...*

Of course he does. In fact, it is something of a surprise that any of the other pupils get a look in.

This is from America, where if anything the sin of overweening parental pride is even more widespread.

> OUR CHILDREN *continue to be a source of infinite joy. Taylor is thriving in kindergarten, and we all just shake our heads in amazement at his development. He loves school, and his teacher, Mrs Shannon. He is already reading second and third-grade readers and whips through books at lightning speed. He loves to go to the library and get out stacks of books... he loves to read aloud to us and he does so with a great deal of expression and drama. Despite his reading ability he actually enjoys math more. He sits in his car seat (a bit small for his four foot, seventy pound frame) as we drive to Pittsburgh on our many excursions to the city and we play math word games ('when you're twenty years old, how old will Monica*

*be?') He invariably gets them right. On one famous occasion as we
emerged from the Fort Pitt Tunnel and Pittsburgh came into view,
Taylor said, 'Ah, civilization!'... after some initial resistance he
has taken to the violin like a fish to water. During a recital at
school, he was actually tuning the piano, a feat which impressed his
mother and teacher both. He will be starting group and theory
sessions in the New Year at the music academy. In case you hadn't
noticed, we're very proud of Taylor.*

Again some poor younger child is reduced to playing second fiddle
to the great violinist:

*Monica has come on by leaps and bounds. We would like to report
that she is potty trained and weaned from her 'binky'* [excuse
me?] *but we have met with some resistance... Monica has
gravitated to her dolls and strollers and (ugh! Dare I say it?)
Barbies. We are glad she outgrew her macabre habit of scattering
her disrobed dollies all round the house then covering them with
dishtowels, faces and all...*

Our in-house psychiatrist writes: 'for a pre-school child to surround herself with images of death implies a latent but powerful
resentment, even hatred for another family member. It is not yet
clear who...'

So many small geniuses, so little time.

TORI *has been doing incredibly well at school, winning the gym* cup, physics cup, history cup and heaven knows what else. In her spare time she's been dancing, doing drama and learning to play the cello. Loads of her friends came along for her Friends-theme birthday party, with a room at the youth centre turned into 'Central Perk' for the afternoon... Maddie is a little star, with incredible writing, drawing and other skills. She made a lovely angel in the nativity play – all blonde hair and golden costumes. The big house news is that we finally felt it safe enough to buy carpets...

JOEL has become the city's Tae-Kwan Do Student of the Year.

KEIRA has soldiered on throughout all this [her brother suffers from lacto-intolerance and her father had chest pains, but it turned out nothing was seriously wrong] studying for five Highers – Physics, Chemistry, English, Maths and Modern Studies. She did extremely well in her Standard grades, getting straight grade ones. She did her bronze Duke of Edinburgh award this year, and plans to go on to do silver. She goes to the gym, does yoga, shops and watches a lot of TV. We are lucky in that her schoolwork is always done first. She is now taller than both Ted and me!

Here's a welcome example of a younger child who, if anything, is even more outstanding than his older sibling – studying at a school which is a 'national centre of excellence' with a 'top 50 rating for achievement'.

WE ARE *delighted to report that Fraser has thrived in this formal grammar school environment, particularly in relation to his personal development, self-confidence, time management (up to twenty-two pieces of homework a week!), mathematics, basketball, humanities and French. Outside academia, each Saturday morning he excels as a teaching assistant for two classes of children who find swimming a challenge. In addition, Wednesday evening's hour and half training sessions have yielded lifesaving awards. Despite bouts of eczema, Fraser has focused his sprinting skills in playing 'up front' for his local football team. Well done, keep up the brilliant work!*

Why they need to exhort their son in a newsletter written for people outside the family is not made clear. Still, if you think that Fraser sounds pretty well perfect, meet his little brother Dan:

Congratulations to Dan, nine, for working hard, digging in his bag of grit and determination at his gift for running and ignoring his hay fever with a victory, despite falling, in the inter-schools athletics championship in the 800m. After an autumn of training, Dan represented his school in the under-tens cross-country championship — with 250 runners his second competitive season of races resulted in a fifteenth, seventh, and in the final race, a VICTORY! As a result of this achievement he has been invited to join the county athletics club. He continues to thrive in the swimming pool, earning his Silver and Gold personal survival and 3,000m awards. At school he remains a 'ray of sunshine' in his

gifted and talented class. At Cubs, Dan is a seconder, has an arm
full of proficiency badges and a perfected talent for getting very
muddy on the many weekend trips to camps, castles and Outward
Bound courses.

The temptation to write back, describing your own children's hopeless results and their practice of lying slumped in front of the TV every night and all weekend, is very great. Certainly few people put that kind of thing in their newsletters.

GCSE *results come through, so it's all a bit tense with our first child*
doing public exams. Laura sends me a text message which says
'eleven A-stars'. Assumed that with thirty years of grade inflation
this is equivalent to my grade 7 failure at Italian O-level. But when
Laura shows me her name in the local newspaper, there is only one
other kid in the county mentioned in the 'eleven A-stars'
category…

Grandparents are every bit as proud of their offspring's offspring:

ANTONIA, our oldest granddaughter, at seven, is old enough to be
taken to things, and she enjoyed her first opera, The Magic Flute, at
the ENO, and Midsummer Night's Dream at the open-air theatre in
Regents Park. We enjoyed her enjoyment! … she has just acquired
her first LAMDA certificate – with distinction, of course – and we
all have to get up next Sunday to hear her sing the Magnificat solo

in church! *Brief conversation between Betty and Toni in respect of*
all this:
BETTY: well, done, Toni, another certificate! I expect your Mummy
has a file for all these!
ANTONIA: Oh yes, Granny, and it's bulging!
    Christabel, the eighteen-month old, is another little saint...

JEB *has been typing for Britain this year, as it is now necessary that*
he use a laptop in the classroom. We have all benefited from this,
and are all regularly to be found practising our touch typing skills!
For the second year running, he was awarded the school's prize for
outstanding effort, and this was presented to him by Cardinal
Cormac Murphy O'Connor [Archbishop of Westminster] *at*
school. He has gained his Grade 3 in saxophone, and will be taking
Grade 3 oboe in the spring, and has joined the school orchestra.
This year has seen a new interest — fencing, for which he seems to
have endless enthusiasm.

Some parents devote many hundreds of words to the multitudi-
nous successes of their children. This one features large pictures
of each child, with a lengthy description of their talents:

AT SCHOOL, *Ferdie continues to do exceptionally well,*
particularly in maths and English. He has also stuck with the cello,
and can now bash out a passable Beethoven's ninth, without music
to read... Sean is beginning to develop artistic talents and won a

prize in the county arts festival this year. His picture, which was
a scene from a legend around the creation of our lake, was mounted
and hung in the new village hall for the duration of the festival...

Once again, it's the youngest who may be giving cause for anxiety. Few academic or artistic triumphs here, but it is a poor parent who cannot find a biscuit amid the bran:

Gemma has turned into a delightful chatterbox, though she does
boss the boys around!

These parents, who live in Queensland, Australia, are so fascinated by their own children that they want to pass on every single thing they do:

NAOMI *continues to grow taller and more beautiful by the day. She*
is rapidly turning into a young woman. She has just finished Grade
7 at her state school, where she has had a wonderful seven years,
with great teachers, an excellent principal, a group of close and
delightful friends, and she has finished her Grade 7 with an
exceptionally good report card which confirms her talent and
ability, and the quality of teaching and the school.

During the year she went to music camp, playing viola,
changing piano teachers, but still managed a credit for her piano
exam, sang beautifully in the school choir, and headed off for an
exciting school trip to Sydney and Canberra. Played the lead role
(Cinders) in Cinderella, a modern re-telling of the Cinderella story,

played her viola in the school orchestra, and received a Junior
Rotary Award for various activities, including community service.

At which point the average reader may feel he already knows enough about Naomi's year. But her mum and dad have barely got started.

The big news is that, after a reassessment of what would best suit
Naomi's talents and abilities, we have enrolled her at St Aloysius, a
Catholic girls' school (no, she's not a Catholic) which we believe is
going to be a great secondary school for her. St Aloysius is on a hill
at Tuckamarra... we have already been to the orientation day,
purchased the uniforms, books and bag, and the dates are on the
calendar.

This is the point at which one wonders whether it might be time to put down the letter and perhaps take up a su doku puzzle instead. Because there is more, much more, to come:

... Both her grandmothers continue to delight in her company.
The last of her two guinea pigs, and one replacement, died this
year, so now we have two new frisky young guinea pigs in the
hutch! Caspar the budgie continues to be happy, and noisy! The
fish, however, didn't make it through the year. Replacement coming
soon.

Keep us posted! These people live on a farm in Yorkshire:

THE STRINGS *of rosettes decorating the kitchen are fuller than ever this year... Jack is heading for the Arctic Circle in northern Sweden in January for a six-month project protecting arboreal forests. After that, the world is his ostrich... alas, we have lost one colony of bees this autumn, after an attack on their hive by sheep.*

What so infuriated the sheep is left unexplained.

BEATRICE *and Belinda continue to make their parents excessively proud. Friends will know that B1 has been in China, and returns from there at the end of January, having successfully opened, run, and sold 'the London café' in Guangdong. She is, also, down to the halfway point in the tedious selection process to work in the EU. This means she has already beaten 3,500 other candidates... B2 continues to save the world, with increasing intensity. This year it has been street children and HIV/AIDS victims in Ethiopia... she has been awarded the Malcolm Deaver Memorial Award at her college, and a Mansfield Award for Excellence and Achievement (runner-up Student of the Year award) for the University as a whole.*

PHILOMENA *(Philly), with her thick auburn hair cut into a very becoming short style (all part of the tomboy look), is growing up rapidly and delightfully and has a great zest for life. Her bedroom is plastered with pictures of wild animals. She has a hamster called Zebediah Jones, and her hobbies are 'animals, drawing animals and birds, reading and dreaming about going to Africa and South America, where lots of animals, rainforests and birds are'. She is a voracious reader (had a passion for pigs, until she read Animal Farm), and has done exams in drama, violin and piano (distinction!) But we are not in the business of league tables, and always vowed that ours would not be that kind of Christmas letter.*

Sorry, too late!

But people are growing increasingly conscious that – even if nothing will stop them listing their children's talents and successes – some form of apology is required. This is from the East Midlands:

RUTHIE *(ten) is in her final year at primary school and doing very well. Listing her other activities makes us seem 'pushy' parents, but honestly we're not! We just work on the principle that children are at their best when occupied elsewhere. Ruthie goes dancing (ballet, tap, modern, ballroom and disco), does swimming, gymnastics, has violin and piano lessons, belongs to a string orchestra, to Girl Guides and to the Girls' Brigade... she is preparing for Confirmation next year, as an Anglican, a Roman Catholic, or both. Artie (eight) is also doing very well in school... the football team he played for last season won their league. Edward is the striker and scored a hat trick today. Proud Daddy on the touchline.*

Sometimes children do have to settle for second best. Here's one who did not get sufficient A-stars in his GCSEs, and is now shelf-stacking for Tesco on Friday evenings and Sunday afternoons.

HE HAD *one lady ask him if Tesco's sold panty-liners for thongs — I ask you! — and another who wanted salt without any additives, and when he found her one, she read the label and complained that it contained sodium chloride!*

Children can bring unwanted distress:

PETER *performing as a young preacher's son called Willem in the rather gruesome opera* Batavia *for the arts festival. It was most disconcerting to watch your son drowned in the orchestra pit only to become the butcher's son (with a wig) and be murdered again in the Third Act. I cried the whole way through the opera.*

This letter is another from Australia, a land which seems to foster a special interest in gore.

HAMISH *is very interested in film-making, editing and that sort of stuff. He is good at it too. He did a week's work experience with one of the local television stations and really enjoyed it... He was most disappointed that the news clip of a fatal car accident he went to with one of the cameramen did not show the pool of blood that they had filmed.*

The whole family sounds pretty bloodthirsty — later:

Our old dog, Zippy, has not been too well, with colitis and arthritis, but hopefully we are getting them under control; she is not supposed to have red meat, only pasta, cottage cheese, and cooked chicken.

> One morning Tom was out attending to the animals when one of
> our cats, Beezer, came by with the smallest rabbit we have ever seen.
> Kali grabbed it from him, then did not know what to do with it.
> Beezer grabbed it back, killed it, then out of nowhere a large brown
> muzzle appeared (Zippy), grabbed the rabbit and swallowed it
> whole. She does like freshly caught rabbit.

The photo underneath shows a family that looks fairly normal. You wouldn't even mind if they moved next door, until you met Zippy, Beezer, Kali and the rest of their murderous crew.

This lass's year involves less bloodshed. It starts off well:

> MEGAN is in her third year at university studying music. Gaining
> a scholarship to sing in the cathedral choir has given her such a
> boost, along with the publication of her first piece for brass band. In
> March when we went to hear her band play, Megan sadly had to
> back out of playing her horn solos because of problems with her lip.
> She was also struggling to cope with playing first horn in an
> award-winning brass band, which she had been so thrilled to join
> permanently early in the year. It seems that she has suffered what is
> known as an embouchure collapse. It is very sad, because she can
> now only play the horn as a hobby and cannot specialize in brass
> performance or continue to play in a championship band.

But nothing as trivial as a collapsing lip is going to stop our writer's children!

Fortunately Megan is doing well with her singing and gained a
first-class grade in her performance exam at the end of summer,
after only half a dozen singing lessons!

All this creates a problem for the parents, and grandparents, of
very young children, few of whom have yet passed exams with
flying colours, or mastered obscure musical instruments. Our
writers bravely face the challenge.

AFTER *reading this, you might conclude that there is little else for*
us to write about other than Jake; well, that is not far wrong.
Although we are busy with interesting work, it seems too dull for
words in comparison with our splendid little chap. Jan: stands
unsupported for fifteen seconds. Feb: points to a cow and says 'Moo'.
Mar: takes his first steps outside… Jun: says 'Jake' if asked his
name… Aug: first time camping (loves it!)… Dec: many phrases,
e.g. 'Ready, steady, go!'

THE HIGHLIGHT *of 2000 for us has been our acceptance into*
that exclusive group, the Grandparents' Club! On 13 August, Hal's
wife, Jenny, gave birth to Henry Andrew Heartpence Turner. He has
inherited all the best genes that his parents and grandparents had
to offer.

WE HAD *a great summer holiday in Canada and the US, and*
Clem had a lovely time, meeting lots of people and having lots of

fun. Clem left for Canada with four teeth, and came home with a complete smile-full!!

CAMERON, *eight, is a bit of a mimic and can recite lines from movies, with a speciality being death scenes in war movies and Joey in Friends episodes! He loves model-making and any card or unwanted boxes (which we have in abundant supply) quickly gets converted into castles, ammunition depots, dens, look-outs, spaceships. He also loves playing with Brigit, who idolizes him. Recently I asked Cameron what he wanted to do when he was older. He clasped his hand to his chest and after a few minutes of silence, I prompted him again, and he replied, 'I am still listening to my heart, Mummy.'*

This family cannot wait even for the birth of the new prodigy. They sent a remorseless succession of e-mails about the arrival of their first-born.

FOR SOME *of you this will be the first mail from Terry and myself regarding the not too distant birth of Baby Brown, the first Spooner grandchild! With just under six weeks to go, I thought I would get a move on with contact lists and e-mail groupings to make it easier for Terry to spread the word on the day. Watch this space, for more news as it breaks!*

Six weeks later the glad tidings arrive:

Patricia and I are amazed and delighted to announce the birth of Danielle Eve Brown... picture of proud parents and our adorable daughter attached.

One month after that:

Just thought I'd take this opportunity to send a quick update and a couple of photos taken of Danielle over the Christmas period and yesterday, on her one-month birthday... luckily it looks as if she has taken on her dad's more chilled-out character. First photo obviously taken on Christmas Day – Santa's little helper!

Can't believe another month has passed – second photo shows a smiling Danielle on her two-month birthday.

This is followed, as ever, by an update on the baby's weight, her sleep patterns, and her injections.

She continues to delight and amaze us, as she's far more interactive now. Those of you who know my obsession with taking photos won't be disappointed as the album is growing rapidly with all her little 'firsts'.

They are back a month later, to bring the hot news that Danielle is now 12lb 3oz, and refusing to feed from a bottle. She has been moved into her own room, and has been taken on a trip to meet her grandparents in the north, though the journey was disrupted by a puncture.

Then comes next month's e-mail, marked by its recipient: 'Just when I thought it couldn't get any worse...' Danielle has decided to man the keyboard herself:

> Now that I'm four months old, I've even got my own e-mail address, so I thought I would send this month's update straight from the horse's mouth, so to speak! I'm still growing at such a rate, but don't have an exact weight as mummy has been told I don't need to be weighed in clinic as often cos I'm doing so well... this month has seen the introduction of a door bouncer...

Presumably one of those elasticated harnesses children play in, rather than a burly man with a cheap suit and an earpiece. The precocious baby continues:

> I also got to spend more time with my second cousin Steffie, who is just six months older than me. It's nice to have another 'little person' around as well as the boring adults and I can't wait until Uncle Rob's baby arrives in August. We're going to have so much fun!
>
> I guess that just about sums up my antics this month. Enjoy the photos. More news soon.

To which the recipient has appended a simple but heartfelt 'Aarrghhh!'

Getting your infant child to write the newsletter is a more frequent practice. It is deeply annoying habit.

MUM *stopped working in mid-March in preparation for the big day. She had two weeks off before I was born by elective caesarean on April 5th. I had a rather important birth notice: I got on the cover of a national magazine after I was born because apparently the way that I was conceived was pretty special…*

This is not explained. Test tube? Turkey baster? Virgin birth?

… I even got to go to Sydney with Mum and Dad later in the year to appear on a television programme on IVF…

Ah.

I got to meet Professor Lord Robert Winston, and we had our photo in another magazine. I guess that you could say that I have been a bit of a media superstar already!

As children grow older they can genuinely write – and boast – for themselves. In this family everyone chips in:

CHRISTABEL: *At the end of last year I finished by mentioning my Grade three cello exams, which were to come in the next couple of days, so I am very pleased to say I passed with 109! For just over a year now I have been swimming for our local swimming club, it is such good fun, and I have made loads of new friends. I am now in the top squad along with Fergus, and I am continually breaking my personal best times, which is good. Coming up is the Christmas*

Disco and presentation evening, so I will be coming away with a few medals.

This letter is from a child in South Africa.

SCHOOL *has been going very well for me. I have started my coursework and have not found it as difficult as I expected... I have completed two pieces, in both of which I got A grades... we recently had a debate on whether migration does more harm than good. I was on the against team and was told that I gave a very good case with witty answers... I am playing the drums and may take the first grade early next year. My teacher is very pleased with my progress. He has mentioned that I have the ability to play other percussion instruments and have a bizarre skill that enables me to play with my left hand as if I was ambidextrous. The budgie is well and happy after I gave him a honey stick as an early Christmas present.*

Tragically not all children are as admirable, and now and again their parents feel obliged to vent their feelings.

WE ARE *finding this stage of the terrible two's rather wearing and tiring, although we are beginning to see chinks of light here and there, although potty training remains an issue four months on... yes, FOUR MONTHS!!! (Caroline took only two weeks!) We started the task during the summer holidays, but although he'll sit on the potty and see results time after time after time, he just won't ask to use it. We got so fed up with the fact that he went through all his trousers, undies and socks that in the end we've kept him in pull-ups...*

Memo to the writers: look, if your readers have children they will have been through all this and have no wish to experience it again, even second-hand. If they don't have children, they will find it merely distasteful and quite likely to put them off their breakfast.

One sad thing is reading about children who have not turned out how their parents might have wished. You just know that ten years earlier their astonishing scholastic successes and sporting triumphs were blazoned all over the family newsletter. It is rather different now.

ALLIE decided that she wanted to go to study health and beauty but would have to wait for another year to enrol for the course, so we told her we would NOT be financing her to sit on her backside doing nothing and hanging around with the (same, awful) boyfriend. So she is currently working for an agency doing office/ computing work. She also works at a posh restaurant greeting people at the door, once a week, and on Sundays she works for a finance company dealing with telephone sales. We are still trying to get her to pay for her keep, but haven't managed to come up with a suitable arrangement yet! She told us a few days ago that she is now considering joining the Police Force. She is also dating other boys as well as the (awful current) boyfriend. Watch this space!

RODDY *is twenty-two already, but still finding his way in life. He's living at home, but not interacting much with us. He spends his time making music (drum and bass, electronica), fishing, hanging out with his mates and having a good time, all of which is OK, but he's got no job, no money, no goals, limited options, and gives his parents grave concern.*

JAMES *is doing very well at school, and appears to be ahead in development compared to Geoffrey at a similar age. Geoffrey is doing equally well, and his teacher is very pleased with his progress thus far. Jill is of the opinion that he is of average ability, unlike John.*

Some are positively runic.

KEVIN *continues to be Kevin.*

What can that possibly convey to anyone who doesn't know Kevin?

Finally, the fact that most round robin writers assume that their readers are as intrigued by their children as they are can lead them to produce the most astonishing lists of offspring and other relations – often without even the faintest hint about who they are or even how old they might be.

FAMILY *news? Aelred is enjoying training to be a magistrate, while Cassie does Citizens' Advice Bureau work; Roger has switched careers and is back at Oxford training to teach German; Dr Bill (Ph.D) is lecturing in German also in Oxford. Ailish, still part time at the Special Needs school, is dearly loved by the teenagers; Crispin does extra mural police work in London; Cordelia (Hons degree, Warwick) has also switched tracks and is training to teach ballet, Araminta continues with top grades in Classics at London Uni; Roberta continues to make her own stunning 'designer' clothes for a hobby (wish I was her size, for discards!), Lettice studying Construction Engineering / planning at Nottingham Trent Uni; Henrietta reading psychology at Swansea and spending most of her spare time with Army TA activities; Millie continues to hold down demanding jobs in the office and with the family; Simeon graduated from Leeds and is having a gap year, in Leeds, Tom is following Music interests – hoping eventually to be in a group – Rose also having gap year from Art college; Stu, now thirteen, greatly enjoying his drum kit. Hope the neighbours appreciate his style!*

The recipient of that letter writes: 'We have not met any of their children, except Roger, who was very strange.'

The Sin of Smug Self-Satisfaction

IF THERE IS one thing that enrages the recipients of Christmas newsletters as much as perfect children, it's self-congratulation, smugness and the unspoken theme of the letter: don't you wish you were us? The message that oozes off the page seems to be 'our lives are quite, quite wonderful. How about yours?' To people who live in a small urban flat and have a forty-minute commute to a dreary job, whose annual holiday may be two weeks in a damp Welsh cottage, and whose homes are packed with wobbly furniture from Ikea and moribund beanbags, these golden, privileged lives are infuriating.

Holidays are probably the worst. Some people do little else than go on vacation, and like to list all their trips in exhaustive detail.

HIGHLIGHTS *of my tours were the antiques safaris to Ireland, but every trip had its moments! Eurostar to Paris started the year where the agricultural show is always high on my list... with free wine tasting, and a lunch of oysters, mussels, sauerkraut, Limousin steaks, it is always great fun.*

Then it's Paris again in March, and Amiens in April.

COSTA BRAVA *for a boys' week was as enjoyable as ever. Tom appointed me chainsaw expert to cut down overgrown bougainvilleas, etc. The reward was a side trip to Andorra, trips in the power boat, and superb food in local restaurants… Galloway in western Ireland was an extremely interesting trip in May. It was the first time I had been to this part of Ireland, a bit wild and woolly but super people and wonderful scenery… in Dordogne at Whit weekend we hired a local guide to see this lovely area of France. The village of Aradour sur Glane was an eye-opener. Look it up on the internet!*

We will!

Next they're off to Holland, where they visit a wind generator, which supplies electricity to the grid and, we learn, gives an excellent return on money invested. Then it's Lyons, for a culture tour and a four-hour lunch with the Beekeepers Society. Lille follows ('a huge success'), then the Wye Valley, and a trip to Champagne where they buy the local tipple 'at under £7 a bottle'.

ECUADOR *and Galapagos was the final fling of the year!… The cruise went very quickly with quite hot weather, animals and birds that one could almost stroke, treks on islands, the crew diving for delicious lobsters in crystal clear water and of course the visit to see lonely George the tortoise… the jungle experience was different! Not as hot and humid as I expected but very nice people and a plant-person's paradise…*

At this point, the average reader will cast the letter aside with a weary sigh and wonder if that B&B in Margate has been booked up for August yet.

These people in east London seamlessly blend their hectic charity work with their equally hectic travels:

IN ADDITION, *we have managed the usual assortment of activities – plant sale in May raising £15,000 for local charities, hospice garden party in June, parish weekend in June, Tom to Canada on a Rotary fellowship exchange in July (with an additional week to visit friends in Ontario, including Pat's Mum and Dad), a 'Bolivia Bonanza' again in October, which raised £5,050 for Lucy and Pat's work in Bolivia – after which we enjoyed a 'rest' for a week in Tunisia, seeing Roman remains and experiencing Ramadan! In the background has been the GP practice for Tom, event planning and gardening for Jenny, St John's Ambulance, church, Rotary, and DIY for Tom! As soon as Jenny gets back from Bolivia, we'll be into the mad rush of Christmas preparation activities, Christmas day with Amanda and Art at Field Cottage, Boxing Day party here, before we fly out for a cruise from Mahé to Singapore! (To get our strength up for another year of exciting activities and visitors!)*

Just reading about it induces a terrible sense of malaise in the recipient. Other people are less inclined to force their travels down your throat, and focus quickly on the truly intriguing details:

ALAN *has traveled extensively this year, most recently to Azad Kashmir. In a bazaar in Muzzaffarabad, he met a bloke from Bradford.*

Nothing more is said about the bloke, or what he was doing away from Bradford. However, it's amazing who you do meet.

WE ALL *took off for Palm Springs for the guys to play golf. Staying at La Quinta, a favourite haunt of movie stars in the 30s and 40s, was quite a treat, an oasis of green with palms, orange and grapefruit trees against a stunning backdrop of barren hills. Bright blue skies with temperatures in the low 70s, but cool at night, provided an invigorating environment... the icing on the cake was undoubtedly when Tiger Woods brushed past our table as we were sipping margaritas!*

Brushes with the famous are not always mentioned with such wide-eyed enthusiasm:

IN MARCH *we went to see Judi Dench in* All's Well That Ends Well *in London, and were invited back to the Dame's dressing room for champagne afterwards — which was good fun, as always.*

This next letter comes from people whose lives seem to be one long round of fabulous trips and memorable occasions. They even tell us all about the holidays they haven't been on yet:

WE'VE *just booked the first leg of a holiday for January 2006 —*

a twelve-day horse ride across the Torres del Paine national park in Patagonia (though we confess we are not camping), a voyage to Cape Horn (admittedly in a fair degree of luxury – no single-handed yachts for us) – followed by a leisurely amble by bus through Chile to the Atacama desert for a second ride. The travel agent emailed back to say: 'Wow!' We are planning ahead, aren't we! And as that is a long way off, we are also planning a shorter camping trip to Oman in March.

Then their daughter gets married, and the ceremony is – unsurprisingly – not only perfect but also full of crazy, 'off the wall' humour:

The ceremony took place as planned in Yorkshire and the Gods smiled upon us. It was the most perfect day of the entire summer – warm, blue sky, no wind and an idyllic setting... the ceremony was punctuated by a series of readings – notably Hiawatha, The Owl and the Pussy Cat, and other similarly highbrow material. Much video was taken – including a most pleasing close-up shot of a guest surreptitiously removing her shoes, which evidently were pinching badly.

That happened six months before they wrote the letter. Not only can they still remember that one of the guests had tight-fitting shoes, they also feel the need to tell their friends about this riveting detail:

... Then to dinner, beautifully served in the ancient dining room with portraits, darkened by time and smoke, of Yorkshire heroes from a bygone age – Boycott, Trueman, Hutton – sorry, only joking! Speeches of course, preceded by gagging orders handed down by the bride with threats of High Court actions if certain past deeds were exposed...

(At this point, I must insert news of another wedding, this time in the Midlands:

A LOVELY event was the marriage in July of Iain and Megan, his partner of some eleven years. They did the legal bit at the Register Office, but the 'real' ceremony was in their garden, where there was a grand marquee, caterers, dancers, musicians, and flowers. The theme was a cruise ship in the 1920s, and no detail was missed. The marriage, conducted by the ship's captain, of course, included poems and speeches, and an exchange of vows which had been decided on by Iain and Megan themselves. Later, Megan donned her clog dancing costume, and performed with her clog-morris team.

You can, I fear, almost hear the stifled giggles emitted by the inebriated guests at this point.)

Back to the family whose daughter married in Yorkshire. They barely pause for breath.

As soon as the wedding was over and the bills paid, we embarked on a four-week visit to Malawi and South Africa...

Here they visit game parks, find a six-inch locust in their bedroom, contemplate buying a tract of land in the Karoo desert, and discover how whites in the new South Africa have adapted to the end of apartheid.

> And then, finally, by train to visit more old friends and colleagues in Johannesburg, Pretoria and Tzaneen, before returning home. We are making a short repeat visit to Cape Town, mainly for academic purposes, in January. It's a hard life.
>
> In spite of our continuing fascination with Africa, Sheffield has plenty of compensations...

This great city seems to have a powerful fascination for some round-robiners:

> SANDRA and Archie continue with their Life of Riley. They took the two boys to Egypt over the New Year and topped that by taking them to Peru in April. Cuzco, Arequipa, Lake Titicata, Machu Picchu and a flight over the Nasca lines to boot. They drove over a pass 4,500 metres high to reach the lake. On their own they have had a holiday in Croatia and liked it so much that they bought a holiday home there. In addition they have started to buy a home in Sheffield.

Some people, perhaps not being acquainted with the delights and the fleshpots of Sheffield, insist on going abroad anyway:

> OUR FIRST holiday was in February when we went on a three-

week 'Volcano trek' in Tanzania, with the main aim of climbing Mt. Kilimanjaro. We climbed three other volcanoes first and saw two safari parks, so it was very varied… on the summit of Kilimanjaro I have never been so cold in all my life: -10°C, with a howling gale off the glacier. I resolved never to climb another mountain ever again, but this is already weakening… since it had been my idea to climb Kili, Dennis chose our next holiday destination, Afghanistan. We went in August with the same tour leader who had taken us to pre-war Iraq.

They see wonderful sights: mosques, the site where the Taliban blew up the giant Buddhas, and the 800-year-old minaret of Djam, which stands isolated in a deep, rocky gorge.

It was exciting getting there, as we thought our minibus driver had done a runner while we were walking the gorge, with all our luggage, money and passports (just a misunderstanding in the end). Then we had to wade a fast flowing river, several of the party fell in, ruining cameras etc. Further on we learned that our only road was blocked by a battle between the armies of two local warlords. Fortunately the warlords very courteously agreed to stop fighting for a while to let us through, and duly did so!

The reader at this point wants to say that he, for one, quite likes Torquay at this time of year. But our writer's travels are not finished.

Our last holiday was in October when we borrowed Jason and Daph's holiday bungalow in the Lake District near Penrith. We stayed with them in Manchester on our way up there, which was lovely, and then had three glorious autumn days. It wasn't quite as testing as Kili, but we put in quite hard treks and certainly set a faster pace than we had been allowed in Tanzania.

Of course, on the other hand, some people have already seen it all:

So I HAD Jim's full support when I declared I wanted to go with Denise. The deal was that I would go with her to Machu Picchu (which was not high on my list of priorities, as I had been there twice before).

This is from a couple who live at a very expensive address in the Middle East:

WE NOW split our time four ways: Devon, Cobham, Dubai and our yacht, Aloha (now being refitted for our retirement voyages). Just at the time I was savouring visions of a simpler life, it has now just ramped up in complexity!

They buy a new Range Rover, to complement the one they have in Dubai. She puts a Mini-Cooper S convertible on order. Their daughter gets a first-class degree, and becomes engaged to a man who proposed on the top floor of a seven-star hotel in Dubai. They also have a granddaughter:

She truly is the sunniest, cuddliest little girl there ever could be! I
was slobbered with kisses tonight — hair and forehead duly covered
in a yoghurty, fruity fool!

How tempted we may be to join the little girl in covering
them with yoghurty slobber! Soon they are off again on their
travels:

The Big Trip was a diversion: encompassing, variously, northern
Spain, London, Brisbane briefly, a long time in Fiji, ditto Vanuatu,
New South Wales and Perth. Much of this time was spent with
people very dear to us. In Spain we attended José and Gemma's
wedding in Zaragoza. In Fiji we joined Sven and Eleanor on board
Romantica, *their catamaran, finally crossing with them to*
Vanuatu... whilst I was in New Zealand, Stanley visited François
and Janie Vorsteen in Islamabad. It was an opportunity for
marvellous sight-seeing into the furthermost reaches of Pakistan...
perhaps we will catch up with you in one place or another!

Not if we can help it, I suspect.

Some people long for you to know just how many homes they
possess. This letter, ostensibly from a mere suburb of south
London, ends:

Do *come and visit us, in London, Paris, Saltaire, or Boston!*

Others imply that the many travels on which their wealth takes them are in fact closer to spiritual journeys than the package tours most people opt for.

> 'OH, WOW!' *is an expression frequently on the lips of Veronica (now ten). Her life is packed full with wonder: 'When I grow up I want to travel round the world, become an explorer, go scuba diving, study animals, go to the moon, become a detective, study dreams, swim with whales and study ghosts.' She and Jack (eight) help to keep alive in us a sense of wonder.*
>
> *Looking back on the year, we are inclined to say 'Wow' on account of the richness of experience it has brought. Some examples: Monteverdi Vespers in Wells Cathedral; finding fritillaries flowering in a mediaeval cloister in... New York; discussing metaphysics under the stars in July with our next-door neighbours after their Buddhist wedding celebration; P. being present at the birth in August of a much longed-for child for our friends Ginny and Rod (former Fr. Mick of the University chaplaincy); walking our last stretch of the Dorset coast path in evening summer sunshine; picking sloes with our cousins against a blue sky and golden leaves background... those tastes constitute the hors d'oeuvre of this year's Christmas letter. Now for the main course:*

Er, no, thanks, I really am full already. In fact I ought to be getting home in time for, um, *Celebrity Big Brother*...

Here is another family that just can't stay still for more than a few days:

No sooner *had we moved in, when Jilly flew off with her girlfriends to Megève in France, for a week's skiing... February: Ivor (with the lads!) was lucky enough (again) to go skiing, for the second year running to Courchevel. Later we visited Poole in Dorset, for a long weekend. It is a remarkable area and was recently cited as one of the three most expensive pieces of real estate in the world! It was lovely, but in price terms was maybe a little over-rated, in our view!*

March finds them in France with two other couples, then in April they have a craft weekend in Devon.

May: Jilly joined a group of girls in Barcelona on a hen trip, and Ivor went with 'the lads' on a pre-arranged stag trip to Prague where they had a splendid time including whitewater rafting, go-karting and shooting...

Not the reasons why most people go to Prague, but then there is no accounting for tastes.

June: Ivor's sister Angela celebrated her fiftieth birthday!! A whole week of festivities ensued, and Angela decided to live out her fantasy of being the Lady of the Manor, and hired a real one in the Cotswolds for the weekend.

Come July, and they are at Hever Castle for a jazz festival, and later in the month they are back in France 'for golf and merriment'. Their son goes on an activity holiday in Kent. In August it's back to France for 'two fantastic weeks' involving barbecues and an impromptu guitar concert with their Belgian neighbour. It is the last of eleven holidays they have had between them.

Some people feel that their trips can only be shared and relished if they are described in quite pitiless detail. These people live near London, and the recipient of their letter has helpfully counted up seven holidays in the course of the year, beginning with Naples, continuing on their canal boat, *Eagle's Nest*, then a ride on the Eurostar to Paris where they pass on a useful tip. When on a *bateau mouche:*

> IT PAYS *to dine at a table for two – the wines are advertised as 'one bottle between three' with each course. Which meant we got two bottles between two!!!*

Then their son and daughter-in-law arrange a vast and incredibly complex holiday in Canada.

> *Why complex? Well, I'll explain. There were seven of us spending our holiday in Canada, Cathy and I; Emily; Steve and Tasha – and Scott and Eva. No, we're not all travelling together; that would be just too simple. S &T flew out on the 3rd to Calgary, where they spent two nights before hiring a camper van to explore the Rockies ... all except S &T flew into Edmonton on 7 July, not direct as*

planned, but diverted to Vancouver where we had a three-hour wait
for a connecting internal flight back over the Rockies to Edmonton.
Whilst in Vancouver airport, we met up with cousins Grant and Sue
on Grant's day off from his job – at Vancouver airport!

Soon afterwards, things get really complicated. They go to an
island off the coast of British Columbia:

Our stay on the island was magical – Scott and Eva, Cathy and I
shared a house next door to cousins Anna and Edward, while S & T
became 'trailer trash' with Emily in the huge mobile home on the
next plot. Over the next few days, we met just about everyone on the
island and spent many happy hours with Louis and Jo, Anna and
Edward, Andrew and Colette, Vicky, Randy and Berthilde and all
those super kids. It was especially good to see Randy for one last
time.

Why? Where is he going? Does he have a fatal disease?

… Each morning we awoke to find deer roaming the gardens
and each evening we're back round for another family gathering.
All too soon, we're bidding farewell and taking the Monday
morning ferry back, then onward to Horseshoe Bay for the short
drive into Vancouver City for our last two nights in Canada. That
evening we all met up with cousins Di, Kitty, Kirk, Bobbie and
Charles for a splendid Chinese meal. S & T, S & E, had chosen a
downtown hotel to be close to the nightlife, while we were the other

end of Robson Street, within walking distance of Stanley Park. On
our final night we had dinner with…

At this point we pray: no more names. We didn't know any of
these people anyway. But we are not yet out of the woods.

… Max, and his kids Tiggie and Ben, with whom we abandoned
Emily. She spent another five weeks with Max and Charlotte and
the kids in Vancouver and returned just in time to collect her GCSE
results. I'm banned from telling you what they were…

Though I think we can guess.

… But let's just say that we were very impressed.

Here's another family that wants to share every single moment of
their travels with us:

FORGET PALIN, *we have been living a life of fast and furious*
adventures!!! Bridget Jones's Diary *is no match for our journal.*
Check out the highlights below…
  March. Having had a great Christmas in Australia we have come
back with lobster patches… managed to transport back ten bottles
of wine from the Barossa in hand baggage, no mean feat… decide
to recreate the holiday feeling with a couple of weekends away in
Cornwall. Tim and I have now been together for ten years… he has
learned to enjoy EastEnders *and* Coronation Street *and we*
own a leaf shredder.

> *We have had ten great years of love and friendship, lots of*
> *exciting adventures, and only two serious rows — a significant*
> *achievement.*
>
> *April: Tim, Mum and I go on holiday to Russia with love for a week.*

But the airline loses their baggage, and Mum has to go round St Petersburg in trainers and a T-shirt.

It's May now, and they are off on a trip to Derbyshire. Sadly, raw sewage bubbles up through the flooring of the bathroom in their holiday cottage. Next month, they are back north at Robin Hood's Bay. They contemplate moving to Whitby, but recall this is where Dracula made landfall in Bram Stoker's novel, and they decide that too many of the locals look like vampires. No holiday for the next three months because they're moving house. But:

> OCTOBER: *Tim and I take passage to India.*

Here, like so many Europeans, they find the experience spiritually enlightening, at least part of the time:

> INDIA *is a fantastic country, with so much to see and learn, but,*
> *wow, there are some very, very bad smells.*

This next letter proves that nothing, absolutely nothing, will keep our newsletter writers from their travels. It recounts no fewer than eighteen trips, all taken during what must have been a remarkably hectic twelve months.

An eventful year! Our first grandchild, Dylan John, arrived on
April 22nd, David was elevated to the peerage as a working peer,
and I was diagnosed with a rare breast cancer, had surgery in July,
finished radiotherapy in November, and now await the
reconstruction route! Otherwise life went on as before.

The trips are endless: a conference in Reading, followed by an
annual visit to Spain, then a weekend in Washington DC. There
are three weekends in Berlin, visiting their son's partner, and
there's their annual trip up the Thames in their own boat. They
take her mother to the Channel Islands, and visit Wales. They go
to historic car races, and David still flies a plane.

I taught at the University of Malta at the end of January and
visited the University of North Carolina in March for a Ph.D.
student's defence…

What he or she needed defending from is not explained.

… To Atlanta for the USA Science Teachers' conference in April
followed by another conference in Cyprus. I also attended the
American Museum conference in New Orleans in May and returned
in September for the American Zoo conference. I took a nostalgic
trip to Hong Kong in September for the International Zoo
Educators' conference and managed to visit a few old haunts. At
the end of July I had a therapeutic visit to New York for the
Conservation Biology conference and saw friends and several

*museums, art galleries, and zoos too! I went to Woburn for the UK
Zoo Federation conference in November and then to Seattle for a
science teachers' conference. We had a week in Antigua at the
beginning of October...*

This from someone who is undergoing surgery for breast cancer!
One can only stand back in awed admiration.

Not everybody's travels are quite as successful. There is an
interesting sub-genre of letters written by people who have decidedly crummy holidays:

*OUR HOLIDAY in Cornwall was a bit of a washout. It rained
almost every day, the cottage leaked and we got little help from the
owner, a grumpy farmer who appeared to object to us parking our
car anywhere, even though he had acres of what seemed to be empty
land. Television reception was fuzzy, to say the least, and when we
tried out the Scrabble set we found it had several letters missing. We
were reduced to buying a pack of cards at a petrol station...
wishing you everything we would wish for ourselves in 2005.*

These people have another problem – international one-
upmanship:

*BOTH DANIEL and Tessa have been on exchange trips to Germany
– Daniel to Munich, and Tessa to Düsseldorf; in return we have had
three different German teenagers staying here, which has been
rather daunting. Whereas D &T were taken off to various fests and*

*enjoyed the many and varied aspects of German culture, the best
our grammar school could drum up was Cadbury's World and a
Victorian pumping station. We did our best to compensate at
weekends, but we were badly let down by the weather each time, and
our beach picnics had to be cancelled. Try as we might, we found it
impossible to prance around in national costume doing pretty
dances, so we couldn't help but feel inadequate!*

There should be a name for it: EVI, or Exchange Visit Inadequacy.
Agencies would promise to solve the problem. For only £2,000 a
head you could give your teenage visitor tickets for the men's final
at Wimbledon, a Coldplay concert, and dinner at Gordon
Ramsay's.

As it happens, pumping stations may be boring for German
youth, but not for everyone. This letter is from the West Country:

*EARLIER in the year we had a week in Andalusia, where Liz was
delighted by the wealth of wild flowers and Frank was fascinated by
the nearby pumped storage electricity system, so fun for all!*

One reader sent in four letters from an old university friend:

*I HAVE been receiving these for over twenty years now, and began to
keep them when I realised that much of the perverse delight of
receiving each year's letter lay in its similarity to the year before,
building up a cumulative picture of a life of quiet monotony
punctuated by small disappointments.*

The woman whose life is described in these letters travels a great deal, but nowhere she goes ever quite lives up to expectations.

SALZBURG *in Austria was lovely, unfortunately we only had a half a day there, so we couldn't see it properly.*

Munich was nice, modern, but not too much so, workmanlike, rather like Manchester or Birmingham, rather than romantic, like Rome, Venice or Florence. I didn't like the Italian cities much, though, they were a bit scruffy.

I sent some pictures to Amateur Photographer, some months ago, and had high hopes of their being accepted, as the magazine hung on to them for quite a while, but they didn't get used in the end.

I went to London with Aunt Phyllis. We stayed in a little hotel in Wembley, which it took ages for me to find, since I couldn't find the street it was on and no one, but no one, I asked had a clue. I think the locals must all go round with their eyes shut.

Prague, where we finished up, is beautiful. Parts of it are like Glasgow, though the main bits aren't.

She goes to a school reunion where she poses for a group photograph:

It took two attempts for my copy to be delivered — the first time, the photo wasn't in the envelope. As it had to be signed for, I had to get up and answer the door to the postman, two times in a row!

She has an eerie knack of being in a place but missing the point of it:

> We also visited Monaco, where we stayed for about three hours. It was quite interesting, but nothing to rave about. We did see the outside of the Casino, with all the Rolls-Royces parked outside, but didn't go in.

> In Salamanca, some of my friends went to a bullfight, but I didn't.

> In July I went over to Edinburgh for the official opening of the Parliament. I was quite near the (temporary) accommodation the Parliament is in, and I saw a lot of the processions going in, but, being outside, heard nothing of the proceedings inside. I should have taken a radio over. There was a screening of the ceremonies in Princes Street Gardens, but that was not where I was.

Some people have a habit of bringing you up sharply and uncomfortably, like finding a ball bearing in a chocolate whip. This letter is from Hampshire:

> OUR 'BIG' holiday this year was in California in October; they'd had no rain at all for six months until we arrived, and apart from seeing a fatal crash at the San Diego airshow, we had a good time shopping, sightseeing and splashing round in swimming pools.

Or:

AT THE END *of the month Ray went to a week's dig at Syon Abbey, in the footprints of the Time Team, which was very interesting, but a bit disconcerting when he dug up some human remains.*

NANCY *finished in June her degree at Leicester, and then went on a three-month trip to Kyrgyzstan, Tibet, China, ending in Nepal where Maoist rebels endeavoured to squeeze a ransom from her of $50, which she negotiated down to $25.*

These people would have a better time if they didn't have to share their personal space quite so much:

FEBRUARY *saw our annual skiing trip to France, and the fun started with the train journey to Stansted. Our carriage contained a skinhead nutter, cackling and muttering maniacally. Many people avoided eye contact, but Alex befriended him by doing impressions of various cartoon characters, which thankfully made him laugh hysterically and be our mate, instead of slaying us with a meat cleaver... during the summer we had a few days away at a holiday park in Devon, where most of our fellow holiday-makers seemed to have tattoos, broken teeth and noses, and cauliflower ears. And that was just the women!*

Whereas these people apologize for writing at all.

IN SPITE *of all the snide comments about silly Christmas letters, you get that or just a signature. Clara's sister Jean died just before Christmas...*

They plough onwards anyway. They go for a holiday in the Alps, and enjoy some magnificent scenery:

> The next stop was in the Parc National de la Vanoise. It is a local market town as well as a resort, so it is a pleasant spot with a good campsite. Unfortunately the weather started getting a bit unsettled at this point, though Jim got in one short and one longer walk. The main entertainment was the toilet door saga. Georgia finds the 'squatters' very difficult on account of her arthritic ankles, so was disconcerted when the handle came off the door of the only 'sitter', leaving it unlocked or locking oneself in. A couple of kids got locked in, and then the door disappeared completely. Good thing I'm not bashful. Eventually they transplanted a door from the adjacent 'squatter' . . .

And so on. The tale occupies roughly twice as much space as Jean's death.

The wife in this letter takes a holiday in Poland with a friend, leaving her husband behind with his two prolapsed discs.

> WE STAYED in Cracow. Such lovely gentle and polite people. One of our days was spent at Auschwitz, a very moving experience, although not as grim as it must have been in the depths of winter. We were fortunate to have blue sky and sun, and the trees the prisoners had planted were tall and green, giving the impression of a rather pleasant council estate.

Strange how few people return from Auschwitz with that particular impression.

But then everywhere has its disappointments. Our round-robinners are, as ever, undaunted:

OUR BIG *trip this summer was to Hungary. We decided to drive there. It's just 1,300 miles there (and 1,300 miles back!). We rented a house on the shore of Lake Balaton for two weeks; this is a freshwater lake about fifty miles long. The location was very picturesque, the weather was absolutely fantastic, and the water temperature around 75°F. The only downside was the food and drink, even though we managed to find Tesco's… the only mishap occurred ten miles from home, when a young lad came flying out of a side road and ran into the wheel arch of the car. Sod's Law! Actually that was the second of three accidents in Derek's BMW. The first happened in a car park, someone backed into him while he was stationary, the third came ten days after he had got the car back from the second prang, when a chap drove into the back of him at a junction in town. So the poor old car has had a new rear end three times, all at someone else's expense, fortunately.*

Do the writers imagine that we actually care about the minor bumps and scrapes they have? Months after they happened?

These people take a holiday in Kenya:

WE PILED *our kit into the Land Rover and took off across the Laikipia Plain to the exquisitely majestic Matthews Mountains. As*

soon as we arrived in camp, a scorpion lurking in Harry's towel
stung him on the hand. He yelled. His hand was on fire. A fine-
boned Samburu girl called Helena ran to his aid. In forty-minute
sessions three times a day she worked her Nilotic magic on his arm.
She muttered incantations, spat and worked his flesh in rough rings
of deep massage, working in her saliva and a greasy herbal
embrocation...

Enough already! We are pleased to learn that Harry gets better soon, but, having fallen for the lovely, deliciously slobbering Helena, 'spent the rest of the week hoping to be stung again'.

For the most part, our writers' trips abroad are triumphant successes. Still, not all complacent, nerve-grinding, tooth-furring smugness concerns holidays, though it can seem that way. Some people manage to be pleased with themselves about almost anything;

As I write, Camilla's powder-blue BMW sits in the driveway below
my window...

These people begin by describing something that happened more than a year ago, merely because they forgot to mention it in their previous newsletter:

USUALLY after sending out our Norton News, we realize that we
have missed off something most important — and this was the case
last year. We completely forgot to mention what must have been the

highlight of last year — being among the winners in the ballot for
seats to attend the Three Tenors Concert in Bath...

Some people just have a strange sense of priorities. These people
live in the Home Counties, and are clearly well-off, a fact which
they manage to imply fairly often:

I NEVER *really saw the need to own a swimming pool, but I have to*
say that, like central heating and dishwashers, they do rather win
you round once you have them...

They take their holidays in Australia:

It was ludicrously good. Day after day of clear blue skies, fantastic
and fabulously diverse scenery, and people who are great fun but
immensely helpful and practical. Heron Island, a coral cay 70 km
off the Pacific coast, is simply one of the most beautiful places any
of us have ever been. Thousands of birds, millions of fish, baby
turtles scuttling into the sea, and sharks which are big enough to
boast about but small enough not to eat you in one mouthful. In
Sydney we cadged splendid lunches off Jack and Hilary, and Bruce
and Denise, though we realized halfway round that we had
completely missed out Melbourne. Sorry, Geoff, we must catch up in
the New Year.

Then, and only then (after a brief description of the disappointing progress being made by the builders working on their house),
does the writer mention the fact that his wife had to have an

emergency heart operation – 'tomorrow!' said her GP. Luckily she recovers.

> Sophie had her ninth birthday at the end of May, by which time Delia was well enough to create an elaborate cake. Sophie is an excellent swimmer and inevitably decided she wanted a pool party. One good thing about spending thousands on renovating a swimming pool is that it saves you a few quid each year in trips to bowling alleys and soft play centers. I see it as an investment...

Our round-robiners are rarely still:

> THIS PRETTY much sums up our lives these days: far too much to do and never enough time. As if horses, cats, fish, estate management (large-scale) holiday lettings, mega DIY and the usual work and study were not enough, the beginning of 2004 brought us a new business challenge... we finally did clear out and set up our display room for our ever-growing ceramics collection. What did we do before eBay? (Apart from sleep occasionally).

These next people lead lives of unremitting self-congratulation. They decide to move from a village in East Anglia to a market town:

> WE WERE lucky to find just what we wanted, and moved in June. The house is an early Victorian town house in Georgian style, recently restored to a very high standard.

The estate agents may have seen them coming…

> *There is a patio garden (no more mowing!) that opens directly through wrought iron gates onto the Great Churchyard. From our main guestroom on the top floor, one can see the Cathedral, the historic Norman tower, St Tabitha's church and the brewery — what a location!*
>
> *Dealing with a quarter century's worth of accumulated junk and coping with all the stresses of moving took a lot of time, but we still found the energy to do some travelling (during the year Will flew the Atlantic twelve times and Jessica ten times).*

These folk have a lot of New Age beliefs, shared by their pregnant daughter and her fiancé.

> THEY ARE *contemplating tying the knot with a handfasting ceremony in line with their Celtic beliefs. They exchange solstice presents — homeopathic birthing kit, eco nappies, stretchmark cream, books for the New Age* (Parenting Post 9/11, The Oxford Dictionary of 10,000 Names, Let Birth Be Born Again). *Tamsin is one of only two mothers preparing for a home birth in the whole of Leeds!*

Sometimes an apparently normal letter brings you up short with one smug line:

> TOBY *has settled into what was Reading's first nuclear-free street.*

Or a smug paragraph:

> THERE'S no place like home — especially when it has a retracting downdraft extractor fan, induction hob, steam room, marble-topped underfloor heating, and, best of all, a purpose-built, seven-speaker surround-sound home cinema with eight-foot screen and two-tier seating...

This fellow has become mayor of the small West Country market town in which he and his wife live. She can't get over the excitement:

> WHAT A YEAR we have had! Paul was inaugurated Mayor in May, and since then the time has simply flown by. As Mayor, he automatically becomes chairman of several organizations in town, and honorary member of several others. He attends many meetings as town councillor and as Mayor. I just have to attend to the social side, and have finally discovered the meaning of the term 'social whirl'. As Mayoress, I have to look the part, so I have the perfect excuse for lots of retail therapy (when I have time).
>
> On civic occasions only, Paul wears robes and we both wear our chains. On other, less formal, occasions, we wear our medallions which detach from the chains. The chains are all gold, and worth thousands of pounds, so we are escorted by two Mace Bearers and/or the Town Clerk and Mayors Cadet. Talk about Lord and Lady Muck!

We've been wined and dined by most of the big organizations in
town, and by other mayors in the south-west, including the Lord
Mayor of Plymouth, and shaken hands with Lords and Ladies, TV
and radio personalities, and (Paul only) Prince Charles. I keep
expecting to wake up any minute to find it is all a dream... we
were driven in the parade through the town centre, and more
recently shared Santa's sleigh during our Edwardian evening. What
a learning curve this has been for us, and we still have five months
to go.

The next letter is almost 3,000 words long, and appears to contain
the complete record of the year for one highly achieving family.
The wife is no mere helpmeet, but 'the lynchpin that holds our
diversity together'. They are involved in motor racing, museums,
conservation, the Church, the Girl Guides, ballet, East European
development, and they have a cousin who is knighted for his stem
cell research. The children spend, so far as one can see, almost the
entire year travelling. This is the elder son:

IN RECENT years, I have not been one to leave my rucksack in the
cupboard for long, and memorable trips this year have included a
lovely Easter break with Mum, Dad and Rebecca to Kaliningrad;
a fascinating journey through Ukraine with Vilnius friend Kiki; an
expedition with Stephen and Rebecca down to the Białowieża
Forest in Poland, a visit to Minsk and to the Basovischa Belarusian
rock music festival in Poland in a forest near the Belarusian border;

and several meet-ups in the Baltic states and in Kaliningrad with colleagues from other EC delegations in the region. I haven't forgotten to go home either, including as usual for the British Grand Prix...

But he appears to be a dull stay-at-home stick-in-the-mud compared to his adventurous sister Rebecca:

This year I have set foot in eighteen countries, changed hemisphere four times, and I'm embarrassed to say I can still only converse in one language! Off and on since March last year I have made Lithuania my home... so where do the other seventeen countries fit in? Well, I was in Ecuador for Christmas, Peru for the New Year, travelled on through Bolivia, returned to Canada (via America) for a few days snow-boarding in Whistler on my way home, before first coming here to Lithuania. In March and April I made trips to Belarus, Kaliningrad, Latvia and Estonia, before back home via Denmark for two friends' weddings in May. Then a couple of weeks at home in June before heading off for a month (via Singapore) in Western Australia (a week down south, a week up north in Broome, and then a tour back down to Perth again for a few more days). So then to get back here again I went racing with Dad and Mum in Holland via France and Belgium, and finally Dougal and I had a trip down to a Polish forest when Stephen came to visit. If any of you fancy an insight, we are having a cherry festival here in July

2005! And if you are ever in need, I now knit woolly hats and socks to order!

The younger son, Stephen, is an artist, but not just any old artist. He is a multimedia artist, pushing at the boundaries of the avant-garde:

> *Earlier this summer, I wrote of myself: 'Stephen Tomelty is an artist whose field of practice extends from performance to architecture and curating and from multimedia installations to interventions in the urban environment. Exploring the realm of relationships, he consistently engages in work that crosses the fault lines of media and disciplines.'... I always said that going on that course at the RCA was like going abroad to learn more about my own country. But, as with many journeys into foreign lands, it doesn't always fulfil your expectations... But I have become conversant in new languages. The question, as always in travelling, is: am I still the same person, or have I been changed in the process?*

Sorry, can't help you there, squire. But at least it makes a change from swimming pools and powder-blue BMWs.

The Iniquity of Intemperate Information

ENOUGH, enough, stop! is the cry from so many recipients of Christmas newsletters. People who in their daily social discourse may seem quite reasonable and respectful of others' feelings suddenly get a debilitating case of logorrhoea when they sit down in front of a computer. How else can we explain extracts such as this?

> GIFTS *received this year have included a towel ring for the bathroom, a handsome set of table mats showing West Country buildings, several classical CDs, a pair of glass candlesticks and one of those curled metal things that expand for you to put books in. You don't see those much any more, and I suspect it came from a charity shop.*

Fair enough, but then finding the perfect gift is often a problem:

> JEREMY *brought me back a present he had bought at Toronto airport, in haste, when returning from his long weekend. It was a chunky metal bracelet. Unfortunately it was too small for me, so we now use it for poaching eggs.*

People can often bring unwanted news of problems at work. This is part of a newsletter consisting of several pages; all packed with detailed information about the economics of farming. Imagine asking this fellow, 'how are things on the farm?', and having him answer in just under a thousand words, of which this is the merest, shortest, sample:

> SUPERMARKETS *are importing beef at 98p per kilo, landed, from countries that do not have our regulatory regimes, whereas Scottish carcasses are fetching 192p per kilo, but our finishers need 220p per kilo to be profitable.*

That letter ends: 'and if you're coming our way, do give us a call!' Or, on reflection, perhaps not.

Farmers do seem liable to be more fascinated with the details of their lives than the rest of us might be. This son of the soil reminds us of previous disquisitions on the topic of arable yields:

> LAST YEAR *I wrote that 'beans were also a disappointment at 4.6 tonnes per hectare'. This year they yielded a mere 4.1 tonnes per hectare, so we are even more gloomy. Yet their long-term average over a decade makes them preferable to peas, which is why we have dropped the latter completely. Once again we have used our own farm-saved seed which,* deo gratias, *still shows no signs of aschochyta.*

Another glimpse into the modern bucolic life:

> I HAVE *now passed over my semen customers in Sussex to a new rep, and have been given more customers, and a bigger area locally, which is really good, and I have recently won a couple of big orders*

such that I earn enough from selling semen to cover the cost of

Kieran's wages...

Having the builders in is, of course, an important and sometimes upsetting event in people's lives. Naturally it sticks in their minds. But that is no reason why it should stick in ours:

WE FINALLY *managed to find a plumber to do our bathroom, and in February the bath was removed and we had a lovely, big corner shower fitted. The bath was only used once in a blue moon, so we don't miss it. We have plans to replace the kitchen roof and then re-do the whole kitchen layout next, but quite when that will get done is another matter. Stephen wants to stick with a reliable builder we know rather than try someone else, but as he is a one-man band, it could be quite a while before he finishes other projects. In the meantime I have arranged our little bedroom so that it is still a bedroom...*

Yes, of course. Can't you just get the stuff done then invite us round to admire it?

But farmers and home-improvers may not be quite as obsessed as IT specialists. This is the second paragraph of a letter from the south-east:

OUR *local grammar school set Stuart a couple of challenges for the financial year which commenced on 1st April — to change the provider of the payroll service (after the county council service proved so awful month after month from September 2002) and to change the DOS-based accounting software (which had served well from 1994) for a Windows-based system. Thanks to careful planning the new payroll provider has provided a vastly better service at no greater cost, whilst the new accounting package does offer some advantages, but at the expense of noticeably reduced speed of operation…*

Or take this, the longest paragraph in one Christmas letter:

IF YOU create a document in Word or Excel and then send it to someone that does not have the relevant Word or Excel program, they can download a free viewer from the MS website. You would think Bill [Gates] could do the same for MS Publisher, since very few people have that — I think you have to buy MS Office Pro nowadays before that item is thrown in.

Or:

FOR your information, this newsletter is typed on a DECpc 425 I Intel using the latest Word For Windows package… did I mention that our old cat died after being with us for 18 years? She just got thinner and thinner and then walked off. It was sad, we never found the body, and the boys and I had meant to carry out an autopsy.

For some people there is a degree of relish in describing what they are *not* doing. They draw quiet satisfaction from telling us how little is happening in their lives, though they often do so at considerable length.

> JOHN, Julian and I have survived 2003 without encountering any
> further radical disturbances in our lives during the course of the
> year. This is not to say that nothing has changed — far less that no
> progress has occurred — only that we are all still living in the same
> places and the same networks of relationships, and pursuing our
> labours with the same organizations as we were a year ago.

In that case, one is tempted to yell, why are you bothering to write to us? Take this letter:

> THIS has not been a year of great excitement.

That turns out to be a trifle unfair on the writers, who can at least inform us:

> Recorder playing has taken a bit of a back seat this past year.

> THINKING about the past year there is not a great deal to tell
> you; at least not a great deal that would be of interest. I suppose it
> was quite dramatic a few days ago to receive a letter to tell me that
> my winter fuel allowance would be paid into my bank account
> within days...

This writer is also being unfair on himself, for two paragraphs later:

I have had a recurrence of the problems with kidney stones…
however, investigations have failed to locate any more stones. Either
they are very small, or I may possibly have passed them.

Another letter begins:

NOTHING *major springs to mind for this year, so I could just say*
we're all a year older with a few more wrinkles, and sign off here.
However, I have had one or two complimentary comments in the
past about these newsletters which I do in fact enjoy doing, so will
try and bring the day-to-day stuff to life. Maybe I could keep it to
two pages this year! Joke.

And a joke it turns out to be, since the letter is four pages of A4
paper. Writers should be able to distinguish between polite enthusiasm from their readers and genuine interest. For, as someone
who can recall the past in detail, this woman does not exactly rival
Marcel Proust:

3 Jan: Had our now sort of traditional turkey curry party.
10 Jan: reciprocal Twelfth Night party at a neighbours'. Won the
fun quiz, and got a plant, which shrivelled and died.
29 Feb: watched Carling Cup final at Will's club. Middlesbrough
won 2–1.
23 Apr: Had to rescue Martin and Kate as Kate had managed to
lock the keys in the car while they were getting the weekly fish and
chips.

6 Jun: watched lots of v. moving things on TV about D-Day.

18 Jun: amazed to find Harrods is shut on Sundays.

Space does not permit me to quote from her trenchant strictures on Newcastle airport car park.

This is from a similarly chronological account of the year in northern Scotland:

JUNE: *Septic tank gets emptied.*

The retail experience clearly has a grip on many correspondents. Here is an Australian resident returning to his homeland:

ONE *anecdote: while posting a parcel, the assistant at the post office asked me how many pounds it was. My reply was along the lines of not knowing how much it weighed. As the assistant stared back, Amanda nudged me... cost! I've still got the English accent.*

Or:

WE MADE *several trips to Ikea in Birmingham. On one visit we managed to fit the lovely new dining table and chairs into the car, but not me and the girls! Mark had to make two round trips to Birmingham and to make the situation worse, he had got home with the table, only to find he couldn't get it in the house as I had the keys! (Just as well, he had his own set of garage keys.)*

The same letter reveals that the writer's car had a clutch problem.

The original one wore out in November 2002 and was replaced at 'Mr Clutch'. Twelve months and 9,000 miles later it started slipping so Don took it back in November 2003. On examination, they said it was worn out, and was not covered by the warranty. He therefore had to pay for it to be replaced, despite protests that he had never had a clutch wear out in such a short time. In March 2004 he took it back again as it was making a lot of noise and they had to replace the cover plate. After this, it started juddering...

This saga goes on for quite a lot longer, offering even more car maintenance news than most of us might feel we strictly require. But then people seem to be endlessly fascinated by their own vehicles:

IN APRIL we said farewell after seven years to 'Monty', my diesel Mondeo, in favour of a silver Toyota Avensis with sports alloy wheels.

I SPLASHED out and bought a new car, my first ever! And am delighted with it — a Skoda Fabia which averages about 55mpg, has low emissions, and is full of gizmos such as air conditioning, side air bags, and a cooled drinks compartment — and with turbo diesel injection, it goes pretty well too.

In other words, it's a car.

It is always amazing what sticks in people's minds for passing on weeks or months later. This is from another Australian letter.

The writer, a part-time journalist, meets the leader of the opposition at a state legislature.

> POLITICIAN: *I have a son called Justin.*
> *Me: You're joking! We almost called our eldest Justin.*
> *Politician: What did you call your son?*
> *Me: Jason.*
> *Politician: You're joking, we almost called ours Jason.*

Thanks to the miracle of airmail, that astounding coincidence could be across the world in a matter of days.

Some people find the process of preparing for Christmas a topic of endless interest:

> HAVE *you managed to complete your Christmas shopping yet? I think I have managed to do most of mine and have nearly done the wrapping. I am waiting now to put letters into parcels. I have a few more cards to write.*

From New Zealand:

> AT LAST *I have found time to get around to typing my Xmas newsletter — you will probably wonder at the early date, and no doubt you will receive this well before Christmas. However, if I get it in the post by 31st October, I will only have to pay $1 instead of $1.50. As I have 12 overseas letters, this will save $6.*

Sometimes interesting nuggets can be found even after the holiday season. This is the gripping start of one lengthy letter:

> AFTER the Christmas and New Year celebrations, it was time for the more humdrum tasks — the first of which was getting the car through the MOT.

Or this:

> THE paper was part of some recent work I've been doing on pre-Socratic philosophy. In due course some of the results of it will emerge in the form of a little book on the subject, hopefully in time for Christmas presents next year.

It is extraordinary how some people imagine the rest of us will be intrigued by the day-to-day detail of their lives, even when those lives are as workaday as anyone else's. Take this family in Derbyshire:

> HERE'S a typical day:
>
> 7.00 a.m. — the house stirs — Jack always up first, Jim or Deirdre battling to see who gets up last!
>
> 8.00 a.m. — Cello and violin practice
>
> 8.00 a.m. — (or sometime soon after) Jim trots down to college
>
> 8.10 a.m. — Emma takes the bus to school
>
> 8.35 a.m. — Jack and Charles escorted by foot to school
>
> 9.00 a.m. — Deirdre starts work

This goes on, hour by hour, until:

> 5.30 Jim is meant to arrive home, and the fun of evening activities begins.

This turns out to mean homework, followed by reading, baths and bedtime. They have even provided a seven-segment pie chart in full colour, indicating all the activities they get up to throughout the week:

> Thur: boys have swimming lessons, Charles has Beavers, Deirdre has Housegroup…

The result is that it is possible for us to know, with a fair degree of accuracy, exactly what every member of the family is doing at any given moment in the year. Sadly, the recipient who sent the letter on indicated that he hadn't seen the parents for ten years and had never met – or shown any interest in – their children.

But some people love to describe their quotidian round:

> I HAVE reorganized my study and bought a new saddlechair (an osteopathic wonder, like a saddle on a pole) which is higher than my old office chair.

Later the same writer reveals that 'Teazel has died' without revealing who or what Teazel might have been.

Many continue to pick over their lives like chimps plucking lice from each other's backs:

JANET *continues her peripatetic experience of the criminal justice system. She has joined the probation staff, and also works part time (Thursdays, Fridays and every other Wednesday unless the week has a Bank Holiday in it, in which case for every other such week, she does a Monday instead of a Thursday, except in July and August).*

An air of desperation clings to some letters, as the writers search for something – anything – to pass along. These moments are from one family in Hampshire:

TELEVISION *viewing has included many episodes of Friends... Table tennis has been less good, with even younger opponents beating me... Premium bond prizes totalled £350 in the year, the best so far, but lacking a Big One. Lottery results were similar, £215... A fiftieth anniversary was Roger Bannister's first under-4 minute mile in Oxford on 6 May 1954. I was so nearly there, but the rain cancelled my tennis match and I never left Cambridge...*

IN TEDDINGTON, *a lot more ladies' hairdressers have opened this year, and a Thai restaurant.*

Or:

THE LAST *four rams were sold four days before Jenny went into hospital. She hopes to have the second knee renewed in March.*

Some people have a gift for inflicting hundreds of words of detail, lulling the reader into a sense of false boredom, before dropping a nuclear device. This is all from one letter:

> THE *following day we had a family gathering which most of you know was a complete disaster...*

No explanation is offered for those of us who don't know. Then:

> *February saw Harry's 2nd birthday which was spent at home with thirteen toddlers (!!!!!) We had a fantastic, albeit hectic time, until one of my friends decided to let her waters break right in the middle of our conservatory!!! I went to see a clairvoyant with Mum and Dad and was contacted by my Dad's Dad who I have never met. I took Harry to see Bill & Ben and Andy Pandy live in concert... at the same clairvoyant I was contacted by my Dad's Dad and my best friend's Mum's Mum... we had our garage converted into a study to add value to the house, and Robert and I decided to separate.*

This news comes two thirds of the way through a letter that is otherwise unexceptional in its stress on humdrum detail.

One family brings what they clearly feel are intriguing tidings about their daughter settling into a new flat.

> SHE *now has her own washing machine. No longer, therefore, does she need to bring washing home each weekend. She has her own kettle and tea pot, and all sorts of things... during one of her many shopping expeditions she bought a whole lot of plants, herbs and*

little bushes, and also food, watering cans, and secateurs... I now go to London on an almost monthly basis. The vegetables suffer a bit.

Or take this newsflash from another letter:

ON THE *home front, Jonathan had his first rugby club dinner. An interesting array of drinks were served including beer with vodka and spring onions. Jonny made it home relatively unscathed, in contrast to one of his friends, who regurgitated in the back of his father's BMW and was grounded until the smell had gone.*

Hobbies can be a source of deep and abiding boredom:

THROUGH *much of this year I have been working hard on cataloguing our local railway museum's exhibits and books. Almost all of them are now listed and I've put together folders of the information, but I am woefully short of knowledge of some of the items. I've learned a lot and, for example, now know what a bolster plate is, and what the numbers mean on signal lever plates.*

This man, who comes from the West Midlands but has emigrated to Australia, is apparently obsessed by bikes. However, he has managed to put his pastime to good use. In 1996 he wrote to his friends (and I have altered the location of his work):

I TRIED *to capitalize on my five years as a 'cycling officer' by submitting a paper to the prestigious VeloAustralis conference in Western Australia. Not only was my paper accepted but I won the conference's Prize Paper competition! This led to two big coups in the following year: being nominated to the Trans-Tasman bicycle planning inter-governmental body, and in the last two months being awarded a study grant to prepare a 'foundation document' for a possible Tasmanian Cycling Strategy.*

One year later, things have raced ahead:

The Tasmanian Cycling Strategy Foundation Project, with a target end date of September this year, has grown like Topsy. A change of government had a teeny bit to do with that. Some very important people have been beating paths to my door. Mine is the only project grappling with an area where policy-makers know full well there is a gap in thinking, with political imperatives for it to be filled . . . all this 'fame' has got us as a family gearing up to what might become of it.

The excitement and the stress are almost too much. Next year:

In October, I collapsed in a heap after having finished the final report of my year-long Tasmanian Cycling Strategy Foundation Project. A fancy title, basically just me beavering away on occasional days off work, but over the years I have gained some praise. It was six months before I recovered from my burn-out.

Worse is to come, for it turns out that the project wasn't finished after all. One year later:

As I write this I am heaving a vast sigh of relief from at last finishing the final touches to my Tasmanian Cycling Strategy Foundation Project. The last completion tasks have been hanging over me.

But why, since it was clearly such a vast undertaking, did he ever start?

I took on this project because of lies I had discovered in 1999 being spread about me behind my back, and I needed to do something off my own initiative to clear my name. The downside of a project this narrow is that some now see me as having a fetish about bikes.

We are not told what these lies might be. 'He is a very interesting person,' perhaps.

One curiosity we have already noted is the way that the writers of these letters will often include long lists of names without any indication who the people might be – indeed only those recipients with an intimate knowledge of the senders' lives might be expected to recognize the names, and they would probably be familiar with most of the information already.

Take this family in London:

WE STARTED the year with an early break, joining Marty, Justine and Adrian in Munich, before going to Austria for a week's skiing... we spent the weekend in Wales with our friend Hattie... another

trip to Wales, this time to see Diane... we didn't have a Big Holiday,
that's next year, and you will have to wait to read about it.

I'm sure we can possess our souls in patience for another twelve
months. They continue:

But we did go to the Isle of Wight to see Angela and Joe, and had a
few weekends in Wiltshire and St Ives, managing to see Tess on our
first trip to Cornwall where it obligingly stayed misty for two
days... David, Erica, Sinead and Paddy are on the point of moving
house... Kirsty and Lance are expecting another baby, so here's
hoping for a new brother or sister for Bronwen and Kevin by
Christmas. Christine and Hughie are both doing well, Hughie
having made fantastic progress with his epilepsy over the year.

The recipients point out that 'not one of the people mentioned is
known to us'.

Or take this family in East Anglia:

IN JANUARY I decided that I would go up to Yorkshire to Ralph. I
had also not met Bill's mother, Jerry's partner, Dottie... in March I
stayed with my old friend Jane Barrett... and in May it was back
to the West Country again, visiting Chrissie and meeting her
husband Derek in their lovely old cottage, and on to Tom and
Bridget, whose garden was, as usual, lovely, and whose orchard pond
Arthur spent a happy morning helping to clear of weed. Then back
to James and Polly in Somerset... June saw us off on our annual

holiday with Charlotte and the pony. Leyla was there too… in August it was the family holiday near Oban, Tom and Bridget were there too… we started off in Kerry where Veronica took a really hairy boat ride… I have been down to Sussex where Jessica's Pete broke a leg playing football… Jolyon has fallen in love with Barcelona… his extended family came over from Oxford and we enjoyed Luke and Jen's company. Tilly is now a fully qualified chiropodist, Ivor is head of science at his school, where Holly is making good progress with her GCSEs. Pamela is now teaching full time, Andy is picture-framing again, Barry is doing great things with the Scouts, and Alec and Bronwen are continuing to police south Norfolk. They are governors of their school, where Freda and Geoff and Tim will also join them next year… Matthew is now a chaplain at his college, and Alfie and Terence visited us for the first time. At Christmas we were 18 for lunch. Do drop in if you are passing.

Only eighteen for lunch? What happened to everyone else?

But these people are mere amateurs compared to some. The heroes and heroines of descriptive detail don't just write; they download. In some cases you suspect that it must have taken them almost as long to write up the events in their lives as it did to experience them. Take this letter from Wales, which is approximately 9,000 words long. Nothing is too trivial to escape the writer's attention – the weather, a bus journey, a dispute over planning permission, an over-priced haircut – all are thrown into the hopper.

THOSE *who knew my late brother, Eric, who died in 1998, may be interested to know that his last remaining asset, the spare head for his flute, which had lain in a wind instrument shop near Waterloo for about four years, was finally sold recently for £410. In January 2002 Francis visited the museum of musical instruments in Oxford to make sure his flute, which he had donated, was actually there. It was an unusual instrument, having been adapted by him, whereby his thumb took the place of his index finger, which he lost in an industrial accident.*

The writer, Francis, thoughtfully wishes to transfer his shares in the family pump-making business in order to benefit its employees. But the path to virtue is strewn with the boulders of difficulty:

To my annoyance, the company's auditors, whose assistance is needed, have upped sticks from their very convenient offices in the centre of town midway between the station and the factory and have gone off into the wilderness on the city's outskirts, very convenient if you are heading for Birmingham, but otherwise remote and difficult to find.

He goes on:

Talking of politics, Francis was persuaded to address a Fabian Society 'Field Day' here on the subject of 'How to manage a Welsh market town'. This is the first time he has been asked to do anything in all his years of membership. Apparently it was

considered sufficiently amusing and thought-provoking, and he was
almost asked to repeat it at their Welsh annual conference.

There is a world of lost fulfilment in that 'almost'. Nevertheless life goes on in its fascinating way.

Our vacuum cleaner gave up this year. However, by visiting the staff
shop at the Hoover factory in Merthyr we got a replacement for
about half the normal retail price, though getting it home on the
bus was a bit of a burden. It works well.

Topics of even greater moment must be contemplated too. For example, planning permission.

All this is being overshadowed by no less than three recent schemes
across the river to create (a) an extended supermarket, (b) a
Homebase, plus car show rooms, warehouses etc., and (c) worst of
all, to develop the site of one of our few factories, now transferring
elsewhere, as a Retail Park. This last would contravene present
planning policy on out of town developments and could have very
serious knock-on effects on the town's existing shops. Watch our next
Xmas newsletter for the outcome!

This is the point at which Christmas in a year's time seems almost unbearable. Will we have to remember what the row was about? Will he remind us which particular monstrosity was (a), (b) or (c)? Are we obliged to care? In a sense it's possible to envy people who

are so easily engaged even by the drearier details of their sur-
roundings. For them life can never be dull.

> And now we have the County's Unitary Development Plan
> Amendments, and the South Wales Transport Board's Regional
> Public Transport Strategy both requiring urgent attention before
> meetings later this week!

My favourite comes from a couple who contributed heavily to the
companion volume, *The Cat that Could Open the Fridge*. This is their
twenty-fifth newsletter. It is twelve pages of small type, illustrated
by photos, some interesting ('Gators basking in the sun') others
less so, ('Mike making a phone call from the A46 during a traffic
jam.') The writer specializes in long, minute-by-minute accounts
of the holidays he and his wife enjoy.

> TENERIFE. *Someone had the bright idea of getting an early
> morning flight, which meant getting up at 2.45, leaving at 4,
> checking in at 5, and flying at 7. This meant, of course, going to
> bed at 8.30 the night before. At 2.45 the radio was doing features
> I often catch just before I go to bed.*

They arrive, and as you might expect, their experiences getting a
cab provide plenty of material for the newsletter!

> We had pre-booked a taxi and were expecting to see a board
> with our name on it in among all the other boards, and instead it
> had the taxi firm's name on and the driver was in baggage

reclaim. We eventually got the attention of the controller, who took our money for the outward and return trips and did the paperwork, 48 euros for the return trip in a minibus with a 'Mar y Sol' sticker.

Their next trip is to a gîte in France, where a dilatory landlady provides more chuckles:

We got to Le Tasceau by 1.30, so stopped for a sandwich and a final check of the way to the gîte, being two hours early. We weren't expected till 4 or 4.30, so when we turned up at 2.30 the landlady hadn't finished drying the sheets, but that was the only thing that wasn't ready, so she let us install ourselves and promised to bring the sheets and make the bed later. 4 o'clock passed, and then 5, and still no sheets. At 6 I went to find her and she promised them straight away. At 8.30 she turned up and we were finally fixed up!

There's no lack of fun while they're in the gîte, either.

The previous tenants had found the Nostalgie station on the radio and we find it quite pleasant, if a little repetitive. Many of the hits were rendered into French by the stars of the day — we've just been treated to Del Shannon's 'Runaway' rendered as 'Loin de Moi', but I don't know by whom.

Each day brings new excitements. He leaves his filler cap behind at a petrol station, but is able to buy a new one. They have a meal out, next door to an office party, whose departure makes the restaurant feel empty. It rains, but fortunately they had brought their macs with them. And before you know it, they're off to Florida to try out a timeshare. There's plenty of material in the differences between British and American cars.

> *Unable to find a handbrake I had to use the footbrake until I read in the handbook about a parking brake which is set using an auxiliary pedal and released using a manual catch...*

They go to visit a lighthouse.

> *I climbed the 203 steps to the top but forgot to take a camera, so do not have any pictures of the views. As it was designated a museum there was no food or drink allowed on site. Drinking fountains were provided, but not cups. I could manage all right cupping my hands, but Dolly tried this and got soaked. Then she remembered her origami skills from Girl Guides, fashioned a cup from a piece of paper and was able to slake her thirst without further mishap. While I was climbing the tower she sat and chatted to a visiting Sunday school teacher who was looking out for things to tell her class, so this was something she could use.*

Yes, they discovered someone as fascinated by minuscule detail as they are! You wonder if the Sunday school teacher found the missing handbrake useful. ('You know, in this modern world it's not always easy to say "Whoa, stop!" But Jesus has provided a parking brake for you. You just need to find out where it is…')

The colourful kaleidoscope of these people's lives continues to be shaken up. The electric garage door is faulty, so they report it to the management. The weather is almost warm enough for a swim, but not quite, so they get out the jigsaw and start work on the edge pieces, though not until they have rearranged the lights in the apartment to make it easier to see. He cooks steak with courgettes ('known here as zucchini') and Dolly compliments him on his cooking. Finally they fly home, remembering to pack scissors, knives etc in their hold baggage. At one point he gives away his secret – he is looking for a special computer keyboard 'so I won't have to carry this laptop around', implying that he makes notes as he goes along, and need not let the tiniest detail be forgotten.

When they land, there is one final despairing cry:

Parking for two weeks at Gatwick costs us £288, which is more than double what we had been given to expect.

The holidays are covered in 4,300 words. And they have bought a timeshare, so we can all look forward to plenty more next year.

The Melancholy Mawkishness of Misery

IT IS A MYTH that all the writers of round robin letters want to boast. Many of them want to moan. Some of them moan at quite remarkable length. For some, no newsletter is complete without a detailed description of every single thing that has gone wrong with their lives. Tragically this does not always elicit the response they are presumably hoping for – pity, sympathy and regret. Just as often they get shouts of heartless glee.

> I KNOW *I shouldn't, but this litany of horrors just had me folded up with laughter. I hardly know these people anyway, so why do they think they can inflict all their miseries on us?*

That, I imagine, is the point. If these were people we knew well we would already be aware of all the woes that have afflicted them. Since in most cases they are people we know only distantly, or perhaps haven't met for decades, the cumulative effect is, sadly, quite hilarious.

Take this particular couple, who managed nine trips in the course of the year, almost all of them marked by moments of major medical distress:

WE HAD *our usual seven weeks in Tenerife at the beginning of the
year, but this was marked by a change in my medication which
resulted in my feeling sick a lot of the time, so we didn't eat out
much or dance much, in fact I lost well over half a stone. We spent a
week in Kent in April with another change in my medication but
the upset stomach continued which made me think I had something
wrong with me. Eventually I left off all medication, mainly anti-
inflammatory tablets and massage cream, and reverted to the
original blood pressure tablets and things improved... in June I
started with Plantar Fasciitis (pain in the heel) which stopped my
gallop but not my dancing... in July we had booked to go to a
health farm, but this had to be cancelled. Stanley developed a very
swollen leg and foot, and after two weeks of antibiotics was still
having to crawl on all fours to get about the house so the doctor
sent him to hospital for a week. This allowed him to take the
antibiotics directly into the vein via a drip. We are both on the move
again now... we are all well now, but Stanley and I are not as
supple as we were and getting up from a crouching position is quite
an art in itself.*

Or take this unfortunate chap:

HEALTH-WISE *I have not been at my best since mid-September.
While in Belgium, I was taking lots of medication on a regular
basis, one for gout prevention, one for mild diabetes, one for high
blood pressure and cardio-aspirin. All these four reacted together*

and created a condition called auto-immune hepatitis, where the
body forms antibodies which attack the liver. This causes jaundice
and persistent itching. I spent two weeks in hospital in mid-
October, and have been recovering ever since. It is strictly no alcohol
for me! As a result of these strictures, I have lost almost four stone in
weight. This is weight I needed to lose, but I would not have chosen
this way to do it. I trust that you are in better health than me.

Some people, however, keep their spirits up and manage to find
consolations even in the midst of the medical mayhem:

OUR holiday in Granada completely lived up to all our
expectations – the only cloud being Sally's limited mobility because
of her replacement left shoulder, necessitated by a bad fall in April.
She was absolutely determined that the holiday should go ahead,
despite her pain and difficulties with only one functioning arm,
and was able to cope admirably… Life proceeded normally until
the August bank holiday when Dottie and Charles were doing their
periodic round-up of UK friends and family. We were meeting
Charles's two nice sons, Eric stepped into the road to view a
monument on the other side, only to be knocked down by a racing
cyclist (little pointy helmet, head down, no thought of slowing
down at the junction!) Poor Eric ended up later in the day when his
left arm was decidedly painful in the A&E department in the
county hospital. He was X-rayed and pronounced to have a Colles's
Fracture. He was then delivered to the Plasterer-in-Chief and we

finally arrived back home at about 8 p.m. after a two-hour session
at the hospital… Charles's autobiography, a fascinating account of
the professionalism of the ambulance service, was published in
November – From Blue Lights to Brazil Nuts *– a very good*
read!

Consolation can be found in many unexpected places, such as
other people's sickness:

WE *hope this letter finds you well and content with life. This has*
been a 'different' year for us, with ups and downs. On 1 March
2004 at 2.45, Simon and Peta were informed that Simon had
prostate cancer. After a few months and some soul searching we
chose the surgery option, and an operation was performed in June.
Simon's recovery has been excellent and a recent test was not able to
detect prostate cells in the blood… It was a shock because there
were no symptoms. We can only ponder over situations like that of
Simon's old friend Douglas Marsland, rendered quadriplegic by a
car accident in January.

Some illnesses are less dramatic, but still earn their place in the
annual round-up:

PADDY *and Janet are keeping well. Paddy has been diagnosed with*
Parkinson's Disease. At the moment he is wearing Darren's sandals,
as he has had to have both his big toenails off, having had
ingrowing toenails.

Others affect a certain stiff upper-lipped insouciance:

> BY FAR *the best thing, if not the pleasantest thing I did this year, was to part company with my gall bladder.*

Or this, from Australia:

> BARRY *has recently recovered from kidney stones which caused him twelve days of agony and three visits to hospital to have pain-killing injections. He finally passed the stones and lots of gravel, and is back to his old self again. Thank goodness he is, as we have had some terrible storms with giant branches coming down, electric fences for the horses being blown down, the swimming pool full of debris. We thought at one point the horses would float out of the paddock, it was so flooded.*

Some people seem to have no luck at all:

> MARIAN *still struggles with her medical complications from Lupus and Scleroderma. The jaw infection has been modified but not eliminated yet. She is scheduled for an oesophagus stretch on December 15. She is also trying to get her ulcers under control before then, to avoid complications. However, she is very happy and enjoys her quality of life as much as is humanly possible. She is finally slowing down her real estate practice.*

Hardly surprising. You wonder how she could possibly have coped.

You also have to wonder about some people's priorities. Take this letter from the south-east and its list of curiously mixed incidents:

> IF THE LAST *you heard from us was last Christmas, you'll be pleased to know that we did eventually get our new central heating boiler installed just before Christmas, but that was just the beginning of the fun!*

You idly ponder why the writers imagine that people they haven't felt the need to contact through an entire year would have the faintest interest in their new boiler. Still, on they plough:

> *Late on Christmas eve, Julie managed to snap the bathroom door key as she tried to unlock it. Fortunately it was the ground-floor bathroom, so Felix was able to rescue her through the window, but that still left the problem of the locked bathroom. Finally, by around 2 a.m. on Christmas morning, Christian managed to fashion a key out of a piece of sheet brass that he happened to have around.*

Again, you wonder why the recipients should be fascinated by an event that took place fully a year before.

> *No sooner had our first guests departed than we got a call to say that my (Joanne's) Mum had fallen out of bed in her new care home, had fractured a femur, and was in hospital… Christmas / New Year was also punctuated by a dead phone line, which led to a telephone engineer crawling around our loft on New Year's Day,*

and a dead freezer which Christian managed to fix by thawing an ice blockage with a hair dryer. Nearly all our visitors were full of coughs and bugs, so I had to cancel a restaurant booking for nine, and set to produce yet more food from scratch.

In February a routine scan showed that I had breast cancer...

Keeping cheerful after breast cancer is something our round-robinners do well.

IN APRIL *Mum, 80 next March, was found to have a small breast cancer lump, which was discovered during her annual visit to hospital. This was successfully removed in June, followed by a course of radiotherapy, and she is now OK, the only apparent after-effect being the craving for a new kitchen.*

Indeed, when illness strikes perkiness is always at a premium:

AILMENTS *this year — nothing spectacular but a new phenomenon is Patrick's left knee. In the silence of the dawn his patella can be heard clicking and cracking like a rifle bolt being engaged as he makes his routine visit to the khazi at 7 a.m. Dr Shaw gave his considered opinion: 'It's buggered — what do you expect at your age?'... Mother-in-law had surgery on her nose and she now has a prosthesis which is remarkably like her old nose, down to the blemishes and capillaries.*

This newsletter is from the Midlands:

OUR DEAR friend Wendy, whose Scottish wedding was reported
here last year, has a spinal condition caused by a car accident a few
years ago. She sought relief by buying a huge inflated ball to sit on.
Recommended by physiotherapists, these are supposedly burst-proof.
Not so! One evening, Wendy was sitting on hers watching the telly
when it went bang, and dropped her instantly two feet onto her
coccyx, giving her concussion and temporary paralysis and putting
her in great pain. It had medicos seriously worried for a while.
Fortunately she seems to be recovering now. Needless to say, a law
suit is in the offing. Meanwhile if you have balls like these, don't sit
on them.

We will bear that in mind. Good humour can leaven the grief.
This is from a woman in Surrey:

MY fibromyalgia has settled into a vague pattern, in that most of
the time I can forget that I have it (hooray!). However, there are
months when the pain, fatigue and feelings of hopelessness engulf
me, and I just have to accept a week or so of feeling disgusting until
it lifts. Then there's the dystonia. This takes many forms, and the
one I have is spasmodic torticollis (which my computer's spell check
keeps trying to change to 'portcullis'!) , which causes
uncontrollable, unpredictable shaking of the head. At present it is
a very mild tremor, but it is a progressive condition and the
neurologist cannot say how bad it will get. Some unfortunate
sufferers find themselves 'stuck' with their head at an unfortunate

angle, and require botox injections (no comments about face lifts, please!)... another diagnosis this year was of multiple allergies, after I had a severe attack in the night that left me unable to swallow, close my mouth, or look anything like a human being. The allergist found that I am allergic to nuts, wheat, citrus, raw onions and tomatoes... my back is better than it has been for years...

Thank goodness there is some good news. Again, the letter would be dreadful if you knew the person well; as it is you have a vague feeling that there is nothing you can do, and a mild resentment that so much unhappiness should be dumped on your doormat in the festive season.

For some people, life is a deep sea swell of misery alternating with delight. These people's nephew pops over from Canada and they have a marvellous time. Then:

IN MAY Dennis got chicken pox and very kindly passed it on to me. We were both very ill and I am still bearing the scars. One at least looks like being permanent. No, I did not pick it – the scab just came off in the night.

Whoa, as the Americans say, too much sharing!

Next they have a really great holiday in Kenya. But another wave threatens to capsize their lives:

I returned to work refreshed and raring to go, only to be told that my job was at risk of redundancy. I left on December 3rd. I am somewhat upset, to say the least.

But the year ends with a successful church craft 'fayre', so it has not been a complete write-off.

It may be my imagination, but there seems to be quite a high mortality rate among relatives of the people who send Christmas newsletters. But they never let the Grim Reaper spoil their lives:

> IN JUNE *we had a nice holiday in North Wales, with all three of the boys with us for the first weekend, in which we scattered my mother's ashes in one of her favourite beauty spots. It was a very moving and positive experience – AND a good holiday! I am attaching a poem which was read during the ceremony. And we had a nice meal in a pub, afterwards.*

In round robin-land, every cloud has a silver lining.

> WE *are very grateful that my father did not suffer much pain. His electronic organ was donated to the residential home, and we understand that the local organ society has organized a roster to play to the residents.*

> SADLY, *my Mum died of leukaemia shortly after Christmas. We miss her dreadfully. Trevor's poor Mum died the previous June after suffering a very long protracted period of Parkinson's disease, a truly dreadful illness. They are both at peace now, but sadly missed.*

Trevor's Dad, understandably, is finding it very difficult coping with the loss and amongst other things he has had treatment for depression. We try very hard to encourage him to get out and about, but he seems very reluctant to leave home these days.

Well, enough of the gloomy news, now for the nail-biting stuff. Ed is in his gap year, and martial arts still feature prominently in his life...

UNFORTUNATELY, *Uncle James has been quite poorly for the last six months — we are due to have some results later this week, but things are not looking good at the moment and he is being very brave.*

We enjoyed a lovely holiday in the Vendée in August, which we would thoroughly recommend...

If life gives our writers lemons, they get briskly to work, making lemonade:

THIS *year of course started in the most traumatic way, with Mum's funeral in Devon. Although it was a wonderful occasion, especially to see so many of the family present at the church, it brought to a close the end of an era, with Mum at 91 being the last of her generation on the family tree. During the whole of the year, following our fantastic trip with her to Oz, it was so sad to watch her slowly leaving us in her mind, when she had been such an active, caring and bubbly person.*

Well, to make up for all that sadness, Janet and I have just booked a 12-day Canary Island cruise, starting from Italy...

THIS autumn was the truly sad part of the year. Jacob's Mum, Margaret, has had Parkinson's for some time and had become increasingly immobile as a consequence. She had only been in her nursing home for a month when she had a stroke, and died that same evening. So sad, but as Jacob said, we don't have to worry about her any more... The church was packed to hear Jacob give a very moving address. Tea and cakes after at the tea-room next to her house, and a pub meal in the evening for all those who stayed. We'd had a similar meal in the same pub after Jacob's Dad died, and Margaret enjoyed it so much she asked if we could do it annually.

LET'S get it over with — at the beginning of June our beloved Shaun, that gentle giant of a fellow, took his own life. He had been suffering from stress and depression for a short time caused, probably as always, by overwork... it has been very hard on both of us as the grief caused the family to pull in opposite directions and we have been so very grateful for all the support we have received from the rest of the family and our friends.

Sad bit of the letter over, let's get onto the happier times. For Nick's birthday treat I decided that we would have a day trip to Venice and have a romantic trip on a gondola...

Here is another letter, in which the most appalling misfortunes do nothing to reduce the relentless breeziness:

MY STEPFATHER, *Gordon, had a major stroke and was admitted to hospital a few hours later as an emergency. They thought he was a 'goner', but has made virtually a 100 per cent recovery and is now playing golf and bridge regularly... the really sad outcome of the stroke was that my Mum, Gwyneth, had to go into a home as she had advancing Alzheimer's and was being looked after by my stepfather. The home and Mum didn't work out so, after four nights, she had to be admitted to the Memorial Hospital. After she was chucked out of there in August, we managed to get her into another home, but she died peacefully there four weeks later... my sister was having tests and then had to go into hospital for a major op. Fortunately it turned out to be a massive ovarian cyst and not cancer (some good news, at last!).*

Things were just beginning to settle down again and we were all making plans for a reduced family Christmas when my brother-in-law Alan had a major stroke last week. He is likely to be totally paralyzed down his left side (luckily he is right-handed). The stroke has not affected his comprehension or speech, but there seems to be little sign at this stage of any physical recovery... Jim's round of health checks ended up with him being diagnosed with allergy / exercise-induced asthma, a hiatus hernia and an 'irritable' digestive system. He reckons he's had every orifice violated this year at least once.

They try to forget all this misery by going on holiday to France, where it rains. Their house is still falling down. But that's not all:

> Cats are still with us but living on the edge – there is a constant territory battle going on with a black 'puma' that's moved into the areas, and our two 'wussy pussies' are losing. It even stands up to us, and is extremely vicious, despite several soakings with my new water gun!!! War is declared.

Yes, nothing – not death, disease or disappointment – can keep down our writers' quirkiness quotient.

> IT HAS been a mixed year to say the least. Our Aunty died. She was my Mum's surviving sister. It was a real strain for Doris to attend the funeral but she did it. Then, our cousin's wife died after a brave fight against her illness. I went on my own to her funeral, as Doris did not feel up to it. My friend, whom I have known since I was twenty, is now in a nursing home. Another friend was very ill, so I managed to few day trips to north London to visit them. Sadly, the first friend is no longer with us.
>
> Whether or not it was caused by stress, Doris developed a bowel problem. She underwent tests which revealed there was nothing malignant. You can imagine what a relief that was! Currently I have two friends who are undergoing 'chemo' treatment.
>
> Jasper, my dog, had problems. Lots of visits to the vet solved nothing so he was referred to the Animal Trust hospital, where tests

revealed that he has an inflammatory bowel condition. The cat is fine.

Phew! But the relief is transient:

Lesley has been suffering from a viral infection of the ear. It is stable, so we hope it will remain so. My neighbour across the road broke the top of her leg about thirteen weeks ago. She was well on the way to recovery when a pin came adrift so she had to go back into hospital for a hip replacement.

We spent last Christmas at the local hospital where Doris's husband was. We enjoyed the time, which may sound odd, but Harold had two much better days. Christmas Day he ate a little 'real' food – Christmas dinner and fresh salmon for tea. During the afternoon we took him, in a chair, for a walk round the hospital corridors where we could look at all the paintings, before sitting in the canteen area to have a carton of juice. Harold fancied a piece of chocolate, but that made him choke so he couldn't eat much.

On the ward, while he slept, we played Hangman, Noughts and Crosses, and I Spy. It is amazing how the time flew. Sadly Harold died at the end of January. Those two days at Christmas, therefore, seem extra special.

Does all this death make us downhearted? No! She continues:

I provide plenty of amusement with my forgetfulness. The one which takes the biscuit happened recently. I could not find my watch.

I thought back to when I last remembered taking it off. When I washed up after the Mothers' Union meeting? Telephone call to Jacqui — out — so I left a message. Telephone the rector — out — so left a message. Then I decided to get on with household tasks, rolled up my sleeve and THERE was the watch, up my arm! Oh well!! Two more telephone calls…

Take this couple who go to stay at a favourite hotel in Wales.

UNFORTUNATELY *the lady who owns the hotel is fighting liver cancer. It is the one occasion I forgot to leave our telephone number at home, and our mobiles were off. Donald, who many of you knew, who lived with us for many years, and was like a grandfather to the children, died suddenly the day after we arrived. Pat could not make contact, but she was very good and did all the administrative work. We did continue our holiday, played golf on two courses, and visited Anglesey. When we returned there was a letter from the Bishop of _____, whose wife owns the cottage we rent in Scotland, to say that her mother had died… to continue the death saga, Mark's cousin's wife told us at Don's funeral that her mother had died the previous day, so we had another funeral the following week… Dennis's girlfriend, poor girl, has just had a polyp removed which extended from the nose to the brain. It was a seven-hour operation… she is unable to eat solids… we all look forward to a happy and prosperous New Year and wish everyone good health and peace.*

Letters in the form of chronological diaries can create some alarming juxtapositions. This family from the south-east begins with the glad news about their little girl appearing as 'an angel (!) in her nursery school nativity play. She insists that she was a "Mangel"!' This news comes just before tidings of mother-in-law's final illness, which prevents her from attending the family Christmas party, and brings about her death four days later. Then the wife's father, Arthur, has a stroke:

HE HAD *to go back regularly for blood transfusions. The doctors involved began to hint that something much more serious than his stroke was involved... Linda and Isobel went shopping on Saturday... towards the end of May we left for Zurich on a Saga holiday in Switzerland – a rail tour. Arthur had more blood transfusions.*

June: We returned to England after having had a wonderful time in Switzerland... we stayed in Lugano for four days in a large hotel next door to the railway station, with the main Switzerland to Italy line running via a level crossing across the hotel drive. Heaven for Alasdair, who sat up on the bedroom ledge one night watching freight trains at 4 a.m.

They buy some pottery. Then they come home:

Sadly, Arthur's condition began to worsen rapidly, and we were made aware that he had a large laryngeal cancer. He died on the 13th.

August: a relatively quiet month. We all went off together to Derbyshire for a mass clan holiday. Unfortunately this was spoiled by gastric flu breaking out.

September: another quiet month. Alasdair and Judi paid a visit to the Family History Centre, and unearthed what may be a minor skeleton in the family.

We are not told what this is, though given the family's recent history, a 'minor skeleton' might well be the bones of a dead child.

October: this month was marked by Frank's miraculous escape when the lorry he was driving caught fire on the A303. He was blown from the cab clutching only his mobile phone, and escaped without injury…

It is not only people whose misfortunes can cause havoc in others' lives. Take animals. These people live in Somerset and have turned their Christmas newsletter into a memorial, with pictures, for two of their pets, including Watson, their much-loved dog. As if it were a gravestone, the first page is emblazoned with the words 'WATSON. 10th April 1996 – 3rd July 2004' next to a large colour photo.

IN JANUARY a friend's dog jumped at Watson whilst he was tied up, causing the left leg to stick out sideways. It was thought to be his cruciate ligament again…

There follows a long saga of Watson's last months on this earth. Anti-inflammatories fail to work. He has an X-ray, and an orthopaedic surgeon diagnoses bone cancer. They take him to the Animal Health Trust where chemotherapy is recommended.

Watson's homoeopath then said...

There are homoeopathic vets? What do they prescribe? A one in ten million solution of Bonio?

... That we would anger the cancer and it would spread everywhere, rapidly. After much agonizing, we struggled through the snow and ice to the vet's for his op. Within a day Watson was already happy and hopping around...

They change his diet for cheaper food, which works wonders.

Never again will I use the so-called top of the range foods. He looked marvellous and his coat was even more glossy and silky than before... a few days later, the vet could not believe it, Watson should not have been able to walk. He had ruptured his cruciate, but was hopping around... then a few days later it fell apart... he was put to sleep in his favourite spot in the garden one sunny July morning.

The whole story occupies almost 600 words of the newsletter. But there is more to come. Their cat Denzil disappears and is found after four days in a neighbour's garage.

Luckily there was water, and he was fine. Five days after returning from Sweden and two hours after finishing this letter, I found him asleep on the sitting room chair. Except that he wasn't asleep. He was dead.

Similarly, the end of the letter consists of a large, illustrated memorial to the late Denzil. The recipient says in his covering letter: 'I have never met the people in this circular, my wife hasn't seen them for over twenty years, yet each year we get bombarded with the minutiae of their lives. I have to confess that by the time I came to the news about the cat, I just burst out laughing.'

How heartless can you be? Actually very heartless if some of the covering notes are to be believed. And animals do seem to be unlucky. This is from people who live in the West Country:

ONE of our sheep is recovering from recurrent attacks of mange (apparently rare in sheep but we specialize in unusual sheepish ailments), another is laid to rest in our freezer after inexplicably injuring itself. Both our pet rats died this year, and last week a heron helped itself to all our fish, which were many and some quite a good size... the rabbits (wild) are looking well on a varied diet from my vegetable garden, in spite of elaborate barricades of old fencing wire, fireguards etc. We have no ducks or chickens left as the foxes keep eating them.

Family strife is sometimes a problem, especially as it can spoil the jaunty spirit of a Christmas letter.

> THE LAST *year has been the most difficult of our married life, so I am not going to bore you with the details, suffice it to say that a close family member died, Geoff lost the use of his right arm, and I had to spend eight weeks away from home.*

One way of handling it is to slip the bad news into the middle of the usual hectic excitement and achievement. This letter, from New England, is packed with news of swimming triumphs, sailing adventures, a vacation in the Adirondaks, an Easter egg hunt, Timmy's braces, which should be off by the end of 2006, a trip to Bermuda, a record tomato crop, and success at the local flower show. Then, apropos of nothing, and with no explanation offered:

> IN LATE *July, Preston moved out. Our divorce should be final some time next summer.*

Moments later, the kids are in summer camp, enjoying archery, canoeing and fishing.

But we all know that families can cause untold grief. Usually this is a topic newsletter writers steer well clear of, but here, from the Midlands, is a letter that explores the topic in a way that might even be comprehensible if you knew all the different individuals involved.

> SADLY, *Mike's marriage to Pru (and consequently, his leaving his childhood home) seemed to be the catalyst for a rift in Robert's family that is still not completely healed. Briefly, the rift seems to have come about through a personality clash between Roger, Robert's middle brother, and Pru, and Bev's difficulty in letting Mike go. Theresa and Robert refused to take sides, but when Theresa tried to play 'peacemaker', she got caught in the 'crossfire'. The result for us was a time of great sadness, with Bev and Roger refusing to come to family occasions that Mike and Pru were invited to, including Kitty's birthday party in July and a lovely family party at Mike and Pru's new home the same month...*

Oh dear, but nothing a nice cup of tea and a chinwag won't sort out, I'm sure. But here is another example of the kind of hatred close relationships can inspire:

> BEFORE *mid-morning Boxing Day the uneasy calm and equilibrium between my mother and I, managed so carefully the days before, slipped and toppled almost headlong into the pool, over some short sharp remarks of my mother's and my impatience over her endless nit-picking about ingredients in the food! Christmas just wouldn't have been the same — I would have missed those gut-churning emotions, timed to return me to the conscious search on the 'path of middle way' of Buddhist teaching, and to remember that 'this too will pass'.*

This comes from a letter from Florida:

> SORRY, *no Christmas letter this year. 2004 has been a very bad year, and the epistle would have been a tale of woe. We must keep in contact, so here is our wish to you: have a very Merry Christmas and a healthy and prosperous New Year.*

Underneath the writer has added by hand a morose footnote:

> *Luckily, no damage from the hurricane.*

Some letters are not actually miserable, but they do contain an underlying regret, a sense that the best life has to offer has passed the writer by.

> BIGGEST *news of all is that I have finished 'A Time of Quiet'! Yes, the first draft manuscript is printed — all 850 pages / 152,000 words. Only problem is that my London agent has also gone quiet. Their web page shows they are in some sort of hiatus and there is no reply to e-mails or phone. I have a letter from them soliciting my MS and an e-mail acknowledging that I take my time, but now only silence.*

The awful thought occurs that the agents might have actually folded their business rather than read those 850 pages.

The next sorry tidings come from a couple who send their newsletter every year in the form of a nicely stapled and well-printed booklet. The pages are full of news and pictures of their many travels and their various political activities:

AFTER *fiddling with it for nearly two years, Reg has finished his musical* ad hominem *attack on the alleged 'character' of George W. Bush. This opus 25 is called 'Bang!' which has much drumming in it. The music is very complicated, but it is trying to illustrate the workings of a quite capable but totally dysfunctional mind. He is working on something pleasanter now, for a chamber orchestra.*

They go to Spain for a holiday:

The Guggenheim is a great building, but most of the art inside is crap.

Reg and Priscilla's socialist beliefs do not prevent them from being landlords. Indeed, they describe themselves as 'socialist land-lords'. This has led to problems, all of which are described in pitiless detail:

Warning – the hell of being a landlord. After everything going smoothly for several years, almost everything that could go wrong, did. Reg thought he had fixed a leak from Flat 4 into Flat 3, and redecorated Flat 3's bathroom. The tenants left in May on the day we went to France, so Reg had the prospect of more decorating on his return. When we did, he had not only to redecorate but the bathroom problem had recurred. He fixed it again and redecorated…

You may feel that by now you know an adequate sufficiency about the flats and their problems. You would be mistaken.

... Meanwhile, three other tenants gave notice, leaving us with only two flats let... fortunately the new people wanted to decorate themselves...

By hanging Christmas tree ornaments on their body parts? Apparently not, but that's the kind of silly joke that creeps into your mind while reading this interminable saga...

... Although we paid for the materials. Phew! However, Reg did do their bathroom, not trusting tenants with this potential source of trouble... just as things seemed to settle down, the flat in Whitley Terrace flooded the flat below at appalling expense in repairs and compensation, as the tenant (not ours) was on holiday and his suits were covered in fungus when he got back. At the same time (and during Cilla's birthday party), the ceiling fell in on Flat 2's kitchen, filling the place with 144 years of under-floor dust, much to the rage of the tenant, who has since left. To add to her woes, Flat 3's bath tiles decided to leak into her bathroom and Reg had to take down part of that ceiling... to crown this, the loo in Flat 4 leaked and, while the new tenant took the initiative to fix it himself, the Flat 3 decoration was ruined for the third time. All this rather put the mockers on our trip to Greece... trying to be a good socialist landlord can be, err, trying.

There is more, much more of this. I suspect that somewhere in north London there are recipients of this newsletter who organize wine and nibbles parties, at which the whole story is read out loud to general hilarity.

Some people lead lives, not of quiet, but of noisy desperation. This is from Yorkshire:

> IT SEEMS *like only yesterday that I was writing to you last year. I must admit I will be glad to see the back of this year. In all honesty it has been the worst year of my life.*

Things start well when his second book is published, and he gives a lecture in Germany. Then his wife's aunt dies. In February his dad takes a sudden turn for the worse.

> *He had been making such good progress on the new treatment he was having, but then the cancer got a hold in his brain. The doctors were flabbergasted. It was only the second time they had seen this happen.*

Then an elderly relative of his wife dies, in the same ward as his father.

> *They were the worst things of the year, but fate had more things in store for us.*

He runs a business matching computer programs to services and products, but this was set back by all the illness. Then they meet the 'client from hell'.

> *By mid-September the relationship deteriorated to the point where*

*we agreed to hand over all we had done and take a massive loss on
all the work we had done, just to be rid of him. Within two days he
broke the agreement, and demanded the return of the advance he
had paid us. He made threatening phone calls (which interested the
police) and set a debt collection agency on us... it has ended up
that he is taking me to court... I have absolutely no confidence in
the legal system.*

*We have made practically no progress on the home projects, nor
has the kit car left the garage... we hope to see you soon but until
then, a very happy Christmas and a superb 2005.*

But these people live a life of bliss compared to the tortures under-
gone by some.

ANGELA'S *partner, Paul, was diagnosed a few months ago as ADD
(attention deficit disorder). He is one of a growing number of adults
being found to have this disorder. He has been put on medication to
combat this. This sadly led to a mental condition to the extent that
he held Angela and her mother hostage at the point of a gun for a
day and a half. He allowed his sister to take Lottie out of the house
after a time, but no one was allowed in, none of them out...*

Happily, it all ends peacefully, and the rest of the letter contains
news of the remarkably gifted grandchildren.

This letter from the Midlands, which contains more misery per
paragraph than any other this year, comes with a promise from the

recipient that they have checked very carefully and discovered that it is not a spoof:

HOPE *you are well, and looking forward to the festive season!*

Cyril faces having another heart operation in the next year, as although he has made a good recovery from the first, it was unsuccessful.

Andrew _____ has been sentenced to life in prison without parole on three counts of 1st degree murder, he pleaded guilty without trial to avoid the death penalty. It is Cyril's wish to go to America to pick up some personal items, which the police are holding, but when we go will depend on Cyril's health.

There is no mention of who Andrew _____ is, or who he is alleged to have murdered. Or why the writers should be picking up his personal effects. Still, life goes on, after a fashion.

We were all ready for our move to Devon in July when the sale fell through three days before completion. This was a devastating blow...

Wishing you all a happy new year from us all!

The Wickedness of Whimsy

Since people these days are more self-conscious about round robin letters, they tend to worry that a straightforward recitation of the year's events will be received with mockery and resentment, and they are very often right. So they sometimes turn to whimsy, coyness, cloyingness, and worst of all, verse.

One of the most serious sins – and my sense is that the practice is spreading – is to write your letter as if from one of your pets. This may sound charming. But it does create a serious problem. You can remain 'in character' so to speak, and make the entire letter a dreary catalogue of events as seen through the eyes of the animal – mice killed, relationships with neighbouring pets, and so forth. This letter is from a British family living in Holland. They have four hens, each of which is allotted a section of the letter:

Introducing: *Nuggets. First of all, I'd appreciate it if you refrained from making jokes about my name. It's lucky I'm not a Scot (McNuggets – get it?). I am a Welsum, a breed originating in Holland. I have exquisitely subtle and beautiful feathering and a gentle, calm temperament (a characteristic much needed in this coop, I can tell you!) Even though I am gentle, I am the lead hen – meaning I am top of the pecking order, and responsible for keeping the others in line. I've not yet laid an egg. Productivity isn't really my thing — strange considering my origins. When I do start laying, the eggs will be a beautiful, rich dark brown colour, almost like chocolate!*

And so on, through her coop-mates ('my wattles will be plump, red and elongated — truly divine' or 'I would rather be foraging and exploring than writing, so I will sign off now with best wishes.') The letter ends with a narcolepsy-inducing chart, showing how many eggs each hen might be expected to produce in the coming year.

An alternative to this toe-curling material is to kick off as if the letter was being written by the pet, but then let them go into the normal human accomplishments-and-holidays mode. This is written as if by a cuddly toy.

SOME of you will know me, Percy Penguin, from Julian's childhood. I am the small stuffed penguin who has influenced everything he has done for the past thirty-seven and a half years. So, what have I done this year while avoiding the sticky clasp of a pink and yellow Princess Fairy, My Little Pony-fixated two-year-old?

This turns out to be a reference to Julian's daughter. Soon poor old Percy is writing in an uneasy mixture of furry penguin-speak and normal adult discourse:

Jayne, who took over my job of minding Julian once he became a grown-up, has had a busy year at work. After seven years in Intel customer support, she has moved departments to become an expert in privacy and data protection. She now works with lawyers — a profession penguins have managed without.

The same difficulty applies to this American letter from Freckles, who turns out to be a dog.

ONE night I was finding my favourite spot to poop by one of the trees along the fence by the Cathedral. When a man passed by, he pointed at me, and said: 'Yeah, that's what I want to be in my next life.'

But soon Freckles drops these candid canine confessions and moves onto the rest of the family:

Sidney's article, about the utility of certain landfill materials for home insulation, appeared in Vol. I, No. 1, of the Beaufort Science Journal, *a magazine published through a program at our local teacher's college.*

This letter, from North-west England, is written entirely by the mole in the garden.

THE highlight of the year was when they built the Mole Temple [this turns out to be a shaded bench]. *It started out as 'an idea'. This was how she (the Mother human) put it when she was talking to him (the Father) one bright spring morning... perhaps I should explain. Since my last newsletter to you twelve months ago, my tunnels have increased tenfold.*

News of the family's attempt to get rid of the mole is interleaved with an account of the arrival of a pest control officer to kill the rats. But soon we are back with intelligence about the family.

David, the one I call 'the Son', has deferred his second year of civil engineering. He might look for a full-time job for a while... he says that geo-technics is not his favourite area; he prefers urban development...

The next letter, from a couple in the East Midlands, is written by their cat, Lulu. This section comes after a lengthy description of Lulu's life, which involves chasing mice and sleeping in the cold frame.

My JOB as stroke therapist became especially significant this year... in the summer, Phil's mother became seriously ill, and she died in the autumn. With all this I think I was appreciated more than usual.

It does seem a little perverse to announce the death of your mother-in-law through the fictional voice of your cat. The letter goes on to become the usual uneasy mixture of winsome pet-talk and family boasting:

Meanwhile my mistress went twice to lunch at Buckingham Palace. The first lunch (with the Queen) was because it was discovered she was a 'woman of achievement' (Wot?) along with Charlotte Church, Margaret Thatcher, Julian Clary (?), the Superior of the Whitby Sisters, and 497 others. The second time she had to say grace at a garden party... even if she tries to play with the computer mouse, I will walk on this keyboard. She has been warned – after five years here, she needs, for once, to sit down long enough for me to sit on her lap and purr. I am very good at purring.

The letter is, as you might expect, signed with a charming paw print alongside the couple's e-mail addresses.

A recent and alarming development is getting your dead pets to write your Christmas letter. This one, from a cat domiciled in Essex, could bring some people out in hives:

ACTUALLY *the most affecting thing that happened in 2004, for the Hapgoods anyway, was that I died. I had been showing my age (nearly eighteen) for a while, and one sunny autumn day I just didn't wake up from my morning snooze on the patio. Jo cried a lot (very gratifying) and in the afternoon she buried me in front of her pottery pavilion (in a white cotton shroud, which made my reception here in Heaven quite a respectful one – a lot of domestic shorthairs turn up in cardboard boxes, which gets them off to a poor start socially, especially with the Egyptians, who can be pretty superior about their grave goods)... frankly it is a little dull up*

here (now I know what she means about Geneva!) and I've not yet
had time for networking. Anyway, anyone who says that a dead cat
can't write just as well as a live one, is simply an ignorant thanatist.

Yes, we can all agree that a dead cat writes precisely as well as a live one. Before long the deceased feline is onto the topic of Iraq and the competence of George W. Bush, winter fuel payments, holidays and so forth.

There is a family in East Anglia, of distinctly mystic bent, who for the second year running have cast their round robin in the form of a message from their dead dog, Webster, who went 'to roam the Elysian fields' more than a year before.

WELL, *I bet you weren't expecting to hear from me any more —*
dust to dust, ashes to ashes and all that — but even though my body
is now quite mummified in the sandy soil, I am not
incommunicado, and my spirit is still breezing around, along with
all the other departed Upper Farm souls.

The New Age beliefs and practices of Webster's former owners make it sometimes hard to work out exactly what is happening, especially as the dog presents the most humdrum activities, such as getting the car repaired or visiting the supermarket, as if they were scenes from a play. It's an extended storyboard rather than a letter. Some sense of their lives emerges from what the late Webster calls a 'Goddess list' and most of us would think of as things to do scribbled on the back of an envelope:

Order skip

Rat man

Write: Jude, Filly, Prim

Ring: King of Ireland [the name of a pub? Or possibly a bookmaker? We are not told], *Janet, Dominic*

Moles

Tackle cobwebs

Chicken corn

Bury duck

Financial Adviser — tel.

Qigong practice

Lysistratas

Clean larder

Drains

Nettles

Aga man

Family tree — start

Poetry — write

Pictures — paint

Publisher — contact

Pheasant — pluck

Arts For All — plan

Iraq — catch up on

Slurry — deal with

Knitting

This is no doubt supposed to convey a life crowded with daily activity, yet with time set aside for the artistic and the spiritual. The actual effect on the reader, however, is more likely to be 'why is she telling me this, is it going to be her laundry list next, and why is she doing it in the voice of a dog which is dead, and quite probably couldn't talk at all when it was still alive?'

But then some people's lives do seem to centre around their pets. This is from Wales:

> A SADDER event was the demise of Pele, Gabriel's iguana. Aficionados of the film ET will remember the scenes where Eliot and ET exhibited parallel suffering, growing more and more pathetic. Well, as Gabriel pined in his Manchester flat, Pele — abandoned — pined away in Llandudno. Despite the valiant efforts of the vet (who declared he had obviously had a good life and had been well looked after) it was no good, and he now lies at peace below the raspberry canes in the garden. In contrast, Nick's snakes continue to flourish, growing ever larger and more vicious. Gwynn's pond fish, who have probably not had a mention in these letters before, have thrived for about three years, but yesterday he discovered that only one was remaining from the original six, and today he was horrified to discover that even this one had gone.

Those people seem to be running a sort of pets' abbatoir.

Another letter was sent to me by the writers, and very agreeable it is too. But there is slightly more than anyone might need to know about their dog:

> BECKY'S TOE. *Becky decided she was going to see me off to America in a big way. Four days before leaving, she hurt her right paw quite badly, while playing with Jimmy on the rough track. The next day it was hot and swollen so on Monday I took her to the vet. An X-ray revealed that she had broken one of the small bones of her toe into three pieces. Because of the awkward site, our vet bound the wound rather than set it in plaster. He recommended weekly visits to check the paw...*

This goes on for quite a lot longer, encompassing the use of first aid by the husband, the dog chewing off the dressing, and the second X-ray, until you find yourself thinking that it may not be terribly interesting in itself, but it is certainly an insight into their lives.

Often round-robinners can tell you more than you really need to know:

> OUR *saddest news was the passing of our dear Sami.* [Cat? Dog? Goldfish? Iguana? We are not told.] *She had become steadily frailer during the year and when a blood test proved that her kidneys were 'shot' and that there was some liver damage, we knew a decision was close. Finally she had a problem with the bowels, and we knew we couldn't wait any longer...*

Here is a similarly sad letter about a rabbit with, it appears, strange telepathic powers:

WE HAVE *had a year of rabbits, after Louisa wanted ONE last year, plus a friend — we ended up with four babies. We bought tiny dog harnesses and extending leads, so they could run up the paths of the garden and the lawns. We lost the mother in the hottest day of the summer. Having taken Sasha and her mate out for a run in the afternoon, Louisa said that it was too hot, and we decided to run them all in the cool of the evening. Sasha did not want to do anything but sit and stare at the hedge. When we put her into her hutch, she just flopped in. I said there was something wrong, but Andy said it was just the heat. (Sasha was Andy's favourite pet.) The next morning Louisa went to let them out at about 7.45 a.m., and came in crying that Sasha was dead. I jumped out of bed and looked at my watch. It had stopped at 10.30 the evening before. I asked Andy at what time we had put them away last night, and he said 10.30. It really upset me, as I felt she had been trying to tell me she was ill, and I had let her down. The battery on my watch had run down at that specific time.*

The woman at Rabbit Rescue [fascinating to know that such an organization exists. I doubt that it has many branches in Australia.] *told me that lop-eared rabbits suffer from strokes, due to the way they are created. She said that to create them, their skulls are crushed and their ears pulled through. This makes them suffer strokes. It really upset me...*

No, please! I really didn't need to know that.

Sometimes the letters are quite charming, as is the one that gives this book its title.

> MOST *of you know that we are great opera buffs and love to have* *opera playing on the CD while we are at home. The children have* *just got a new hamster, and we have noticed that whenever we play* *Verdi or Mozart or Wagner, he sits still, doing nothing or just* *nibbling on his food. But whenever we play Puccini, he leaps onto* *his wheel and starts spinning joyfully.* One Fine Day, *or* Your Tiny Hand, *all get him going.* On With The Motley *or the* Liebestod *just leave him cold.*

A slight element of excusable exaggeration there, I suspect.

Many people find that the muse of poetry comes knocking at their door in the festive season. She should always be sent away, without so much as a mince-pie. She is not welcome. She leads to stuff like this, from the American West:

> THIS *year brought us blessings which we will tell,* *Doug's recovery from surgery last December went well,* *As to Belinda and Dad's head-on crash with the car,* *We're thankful their injuries weren't worse by far...*
>
> *April found us in England with sister-in-law Pru,* *Where to visit her mother in Exeter we flew.*

We walked on the footpaths and hiked on the moor,
And met the wonderful people of England, for sure...

At this point they run out of rhymes, or perhaps just children, and are reduced to a shortened verse:

Jacqui's doing her Masters at San Francisco State,
Darlene's research continues on yeast's DNA trait,
While Jan's work is a challenge, in Boston, as of late.

Our greatest blessings we saved for the last —
Our family increased by two in the six months past.
Warren Randolph's birth was the 30th of May,
To Dirk and Connie, at eight pounds did he weigh.

For many people, cramming the required number of syllables into each line, as well as finding rhymes, is just too difficult. Others manage to get the scansion more or less right, though the effect can be ruined by the banality of the material. T. S. Eliot could write about lunch in a hotel; the rest of us are less felicitous:

Now *Jack is manager of the bar in Leeds's Stafford Hotel,*
And Hattie has a part time job there, waitressing, as well.
She's nearly finished her degree; hotel management will be new,
So together they are hoping that their dream will soon come
true...

Stephen and his partner, Miranda is her name,
Still spend their time on DIY, no room is now the same.
They've even done the garden, which used to be so bare,
But now it's full of flowers and trees with Miranda's tender care.
'Do come and see us, Mum and Dad, because we have no car.
We need to go to B&Q, it isn't very far.'

These people from Australia stretch the poetic form to its very limit:

THERE was a 'young' couple from 'Strayya
Who decided to go right awayya
To England and Wales
And Scotland and a-else,
To see family and those much, much grayya...

On returning to Oz,
They stopped off, because
Japan, specially Kyoto, said 'hiyya!'
The temples were 'Wow!!!'
The bullet train — 'POW!!!'
But a day — far too short — for a stayya.

At this point, inspiration deserts them and they return to prose:

They've just seen their builder,
With persuasion have willed a
Nice draughtsman to draw up some initial floor plans and

---

*elevations as the first step to finalizing the details and submitting
the official plans to the council.*

And back again:

Next summer — out here,
(Construction so near)
Our new home will be happening — just 'cos!

But that is no more bold and unconventional than these people
who write in free verse, making an agreeable change.

IN *summer we camped alone in a woodland yurt where peace came*
                                                            dripping slow,
Long walks in autumn.
Rams tupped the ewes.
Spotty died.
Tick and Boo came to stay.
Francis and Sarah got married.
Even under heavy snow we see snowdrops and some new growth.
In the East we saw rhubarb already.
In the summer we eat cucumbers.

The last line has a fine elegiac ring.

Some people send verses designed to cheer up the recipient,
though one fears it might have the opposite effect. This is also
from Australia:

SMILING *is infectious,*
You catch it like the 'flu,
When someone smiled at me today,
I started smiling too.

I passed around the corner and someone saw my grin.
When he smiled I realized I'd passed it onto him.

I thought about that smile, then I realized its worth.
A single smile, just like mine, could travel round the earth.

So, if you feel a smile begin, don't leave it undetected.
Let's start an epidemic quick, and get the world infected!

Reading that can leave you with a rictus grimace, strangely similar to, yet very different from a smile.

One family sent their news in the form of a crossword, which can only be solved if you know the answers already. As the recipient says, 'We are supposed to know the family's life in all its ghastly detail and spend time trying to sort out the clues and answers.' And the clues are quite baffling: 'Thereby hangs a tail (in our house) (4)'. What is that – the name of a pet? 'Two pigs of this kind have recently joined our household (6)'; 'We love to play this game together (6)'; 'One route to our newly renovated attic (4,4)' What can that be? Roof lift? Rope pull? I suppose you could squeeze in 'loft ladder' if you wrote really small. 'Airport we have never flown from (5)'. Who can possibly guess? Luton? Paris? Quito?

Why on earth should anyone want a Christmas newsletter that only tells you what the news is if you already know it?

Some people, possibly in response to the mockery evoked these days by round robins, have begun to send very short ones.

> A BRIEF *summary of the year: Madeleine gave birth to Scarlett (1st July), Edward moved jobs (to Nottingham), Edward eventually became Dr Edward, we all moved house.*

Or this, from a reader:

> WE HAVE *received what may possibly the shortest Christmas letter we have ever received. We have not heard from these people since last Christmas. It reads entirely 'Henry has broken his arm'. After some thought, we realized that Henry's wife was writing the cards this year for the first time.*

Some are just sad:

> SORRY, *no newsletter this year, as we lost my sister Josie in September. Best wishes for the festive season.*

One especially poignant letter reads, in its entirety:

> *2004. Don't even ask.*

Some are genuinely funny. I liked this spoof from California:

> KYLE *took down our boxes of antique decorations late last night from the attic. The mice had eaten them all! But the good news is*

that a window in the attic had been open and the mice had all
frozen to death. The mice are remarkably preserved and look so cute,
we are going to use them as decorations this year. Aren't we
creative?

This is from a Welsh family, writing about their life and thoughts
on current events:

THERE *are many eccentricities in British politics, but the oddest of*
the lot must be the Liberal Democrat who was sacked as a
frontbench spokesman when she said that if she were a Palestinian,
she might become a suicide bomber herself. Less widely reported was
that a Palestinian suicide bomber had caused equal outrage by
saying that if she were British, she might just become a Liberal
Democrat MP. She was called in by the Hamas chief whip, and had
her bomb withdrawn...

Some are simply baffling:

TOM *informs the world that his current thesis topic is in the area*
of cyborg research (artificial bone replacements) and that he is still
going by the pseudonym Ethel. He maintains a fairly active online
presence, and can be contacted at EthelTheHut@btinternet.com
for those truly desperate to get in touch with him.

This is part of a long letter from a Welsh gay. It includes cheery
descriptions of trips to Budapest, London, Helsinki, Estonia and
Tenerife. He also goes off walking with a Welsh gay rambling asso-

ciation, which has managed to get special permission to traverse
land owned by the Ministry of Defence.

> OUR group was the first to sample some very beautiful scenery. We
> still needed MoD permission and we were warned not to pick
> anything up. I nearly asked 'do you mean unexploded grenades, or
> 16-year-old squaddies? Well, both can go off in yer hand!'

Thank you for that. I think we'll finish there.

The Sophistry of Sanctimony

'How is it,' asks one of my correspondents, 'that everything good that happens can be credited to God, but He is in no way to blame for the bad things?' It is something of a mystery, often apparent but rarely explained, in a sub-genre of the Christmas round robin – the letter of praise and thanksgiving. For some people the news of their lives over the previous twelve months merely serves as top dressing for the real business: the message of Jesus Christ.

One is loath to make fun of people's religion, but it is sometimes strange that suffering the most horrible illness will actually strengthen people's faith, while never once leaving them to question how they were allowed to become ill in the first place.

Some are unexceptional, making parts of their letters merely seem like the peroration in a rather dreary C of E sermon:

> So, another year gone, another year older. Probably not wiser, but a
> wide range of experiences to look back on with joy, sadness,
> frustration or simply fondness. Most importantly, however, we look
> forward to the annual but always fresh celebration of the birth of
> Christ. Undimmed by repeated carol services, or the frustrations of
> church politics, we can still join with the angels and experience
> afresh the message of goodwill and the promise of salvation,

*brought especially at Christmas, but with us forever... our prayers
are with you.*

Some make their entire letter a hymn to the Lord. This one, from
a doctor's family in the south-east, is decorated with texts, apparently thrown in at random:

> ... THE *wedding dress is bought, and plans are already well
> advanced, as you can imagine. Jesus said 'I am the light of the
> world'... real advances have been made in developing national
> guidelines and standards for patients in A&E departments. The
> Executive Committee has also been a good experience. Life is full of
> joy and challenge but we only have one life to give, just as Jesus
> only had one life to give. He gave his life for us, so let us give our
> life for Him...*

The wife, Janet, takes over the narration:

> *I have managed to travel overseas fourteen times for one purpose or
> another in the last twelve months. It has been an exhilarating
> experience, which leaves me with the question: 'Lord, what do you
> want me to do with my time?'*

She ruptures an Achilles tendon while playing squash in February,
so the answer to that question seems to be 'lie in bed in a plaster
cast'. One of their daughters is a midwife, and is going to Thailand
for the purpose of rescuing young prostitutes, 'getting them off
the streets and giving them a future in Jesus (and a different job!).'

The family goes to the Bahamas for a holiday:

This was nearly a disaster, due to the hurricane, but God had mercy on us and managed to rearrange the whole thing in the last two days before departure.

Does she seriously believe that God rearranged the path of the hurricane purely in order to avoid spoiling their holiday? Or is this Janet's ever so subtle jibe at the rest of the family? It is impossible to know. Or take this:

June saw me operated on for gall-bladder removal. The surgeon said it took a bottle of whisky that evening to help him get over it. Evidently, when he got 'in there' he found adhesions from former operations, and he had to fillet his way through to get a gall bladder. With prayer support as I had, he could not fail. I still sport a lovely long red scar across my tum…

That letter, dated December 2004, also includes the surprising but apparently true fact that they have a granddaughter in Australia whose parents named her, some time before Boxing Day 2004, 'Tsunami'.

But it is quite clear that, for religious folk, even if God doesn't prevent them from becoming ill, He moves promptly into action when they are:

AROUND the same time, some fleeting symptoms prompted Norman to visit the GP. It was lucky he did, because the symptoms lasted thirty-six hours. In May, he was diagnosed with kidney cancer. Unbelievably, we had only one sleepless night, punctuated by numerous nocturnal cups of tea. We then realized that in a wonderful way we are being looked after. People from all round the world prayed for Norman, and our faith convinced us that things would continue to go well.

The hospital invited Norman to spend ten to fourteen days recovering from surgery, but they had had enough after three days and sent him home — minus his right kidney and its 'hanger-on'. Apparently this was a record. He didn't even miss one Sunday at our local church, and caused one poor old lady to fall off her seat when he reappeared much earlier than expected!

These people seem to have rediscovered Christian Science. After the usual round of house conversions and successful children, the wife writes:

I HAVE *been organizing Christian conferences on 'Creativity — Restoring the Soul'; 'The Prophetic' and 'Restoration Healing'. The numbers attending have increased each time and we are expecting a hundred in February for a Healing Conference. It has been wonderful and so rewarding to see people released from fears, bondages, trauma, etc.*

The highlight of my year was when another friend and myself prayed for a woman, Annie, who had Multiple Chemical Allergy and had been confined to one room for five to six years. A ghastly

'modern' disease in which people are allergic to any type of
chemical smell, including soap, hairspray, cleaning fluids, etc.
Anyway, the Lord completely healed her!! Six months later
she is still extremely well and enjoying a normal life.
Hallelujah!

Or take this:

KATIE'*s seasonal entertainment job has finished for now, so she is*
selling shoes in faith, at Debenhams, and loving it!!! She buys just
as many as she sells.

Which leaves you to wonder how you sell shoes in faith. 'Madam
might prefer this hard-wearing style; it has an immortal sole,'
perhaps. (An apology: I have just been told that 'faith' is a shoe-
store within Debenhams.) The letter goes on:

Sadly, one of my girl pupils, Vienna, was killed in a car crash while
celebrating her ninth birthday in New Zealand, visiting Jake, her
big brother, who was on a gap year there. Sadly Jake was driving.
Tania, their mother, is still wearing a metal contraption on her
head. The children and I had a memorial service for Vienna, and my
headteacher actually praised me! As Tania and Jake approach their
first Christmas since Vienna's death, I would ask my Christian
friends to pray for them, please.

Oh dear, one doesn't want to be cynical, but it does appear that
faith can be a kind of WD-40, to be sprayed onto all of life's dif-

ficulties, great and small. True faith seems to involve attributing almost every good thing in your life to the Lord's beneficent help:

> SPEAKING *of co-incidences, or God's hand, Chery was on a plane going to Chicago for a business meeting, and guess who the flight attendant was? Tiffany Bayliss, her aunt!*

Religious people find religion everywhere they go.

> WHEN *I walked down our main shopping street on Victorian Night, I was very impressed by a group of youngsters about seventeen to nineteen years old playing music and singing the songs I have on my latest worship tape in the car... Tamsin, my shyest daughter, has just started a Christian Union course and her non-Christian friends go along.*

This letter, from north-west England, is a chapter of medical mayhem, relieved only by religious faith:

> IT HAS *been a very strange year for Harold and myself. In March he woke up one morning with chest pains and was taken to hospital, where I was told he was having a heart attack! All I could think was, I can't believe this is happening. I cried out to Father God, who saw my tears and heard my prayer for help. I felt His comfort and knew His peace. If you have time, read Psalm 25. Harold said he was at peace all the time, and kept repeating Psalm 25. I don't honestly know how people manage without faith in a Living God!*
>
> *After four days of intensive care, Harold was allowed home, with*

*the verdict possibly angina. A few weeks later his father, aged
ninety-one, died and my mother fell and bruised her hip. She
couldn't walk and had to use a wheelchair. We cancelled our
holidays around the Greek islands… a few months later Harold
was waiting to cross the road and a van ran right into the back of
him, causing whiplash and a written-off van!*

*We must not expect life to be just. Christianity does not teach
that it is; we live in a fallen world, and our prayer should not be for
justice in life, but for God's help to turn every pain into a pearl. On
a brighter note our grandchildren, Toby and Cameron, are very much
involved in football… and enjoying all the beauty God has created.*

It can be slightly alarming to discover whole families of devout
people. Don't the children ever get tempted to cut loose and let
rip? Only up to a point. These people from the north-east have
each member of the family make a contribution, starting with the
wife, who had heart problems:

IT *took the following five weeks off work to accept that doing three
jobs, plus being a Mum, wife, preacher and popular agony aunt for
a year could constitute 'stress'.*

His faith helps her husband through it all.

*Walking, praying weekly, with a friend and psychotherapy have
been anchors in the storm…*

Their older boy starts by sounding like any other teenager:

The last year has been great for me! In January I became interested in Warhammer 40,000. This is a battle game set in the 41st millennium. I have been collecting an army of Chaos Space Marines. I then went on to discover P.O.D., a Christian metal band, and have had loads of fun listening to them. Harvest, a Christian youth camp, has been a great help spiritually, and a chance to get away from Mum and Dad... school has been tiring, but God, Mum, Dad and my brother have helped me pull through.

His younger brother reports an interest in skateboarding and rugby.

It was my first year at Harvest this year. Boy, it was great! Just a few days ago I was at a Christian rock concert called ixth hour *(ninth hour). This, combined with Harvest, have made me (a) wonderfully refreshed in God's spirit, and (b) extremely tired.*

For some people, God's involvement in their life is merely an extension of every other satisfactory circumstance, such as the promotion at work, the talents of their offspring, and the new water feature in the garden. These people have a wonderful holiday in Brazil.

IN RIO, we goggled at the views and the huge, famous statue of Christ the Redeemer, nail prints and all, another moving experience... on our last day we bravely went up in cable cars and near the top we could hear singing — former members of Yale's

*choral society were on tour. As the sun went down, the clouds parted
and the Christ appeared, and with the singing in the background,
that was a very special moment. The Lord had been so good to us
throughout the trip.*

Would that be the same Lord that arranged for the earlier couple
to cancel their Greek holiday because of family illness?

One reader writes in exasperation from the Home Counties:

My *all-time favourite letter came from an old university friend
who is now a born-again Christian. Annually we get to hear of
God's purpose in their lives, though He wasn't responsible for their
eldest son being mugged. That's the trouble with Christianity — it is
never God's fault. Anyway, the classic sentence (I no longer have the
original) refers to some happy-clappy musical they put on at their
church:*

*'I never thought I would dance in church, but God had other
ideas!'*

Aaargh!

Some of the scarier letters come from the United States. This, for
example, is from an American air force family, and most of it
consists of reunions, trips to visit old military friends, holidays and
funerals. Then suddenly:

With *the Episcopal church in the USA in freefall towards the
fellow with red horns, the Church of Christ the King is a refreshing*

island in a sea of effluent. God willing, it will stay that way. We
assume with the new election of a heretic to the San Diego Bishop's
office, the final battle may be sooner rather than later.

That sounds a little threatening.

Some people are into a form of vague, miasmic mysticism.
This, not surprisingly perhaps, is from California:

In 2005, we enter the twenty-second year of our Mystery School.
How about that? Twenty-two years of continuous adventures and
journeys of mind, body and spirit into the mystery of who and what
we are, and what we yet may be. Twenty-two years of a bonded,
cherishing community and training in what makes life worthwhile.
Twenty-two years of what many have called the best school in the
world.

Many have lost their sense of who, why and what we are in the
face of so many challenges for which most of us have been
unprepared. Our purpose and destiny are shrouded in mystery, and
it will take the hardy traveler into the mind and soul's deepest
continents to rediscover the path that leads to the greening of this
world and time. This is why the Mystery School is dedicated to the
new journey of our lives, during which we will find the maps
and enter together into the places where our deepest purposes
touch the emergent new story that is struggling to enter into
time...

What's that? Sorry, I was miles away…

This is from a woman in New York City who doesn't waste much time in getting down to the spiritual sales pitch.

> … I ALSO *continue to sing in the Voices of Unity and have begun a two-year interfaith seminary program. What is interfaith, you may ask? It is the study of all religions in order to understand our commonalities rather than our differences. At this time, it is more necessary than ever. If you believe this is something worthwhile and wish to contribute to the study and to my work in it, you can make an end of the tax year write-off to One Spirit Interfaith, and send it to me.*

At least she doesn't include a tear-off slip at the bottom.

The final letter in this section is extraordinary. It is approximately 6,200 words long and comes from a British family now farming in New Zealand. Indeed, it is so long that it could easily serve as an instruction manual for anyone setting up a farm in New Zealand, blended seamlessly with a devotional volume about God's goodness.

For He is everywhere.

> WE *are most grateful to our family for the wonderful day they organized, and we are keenly looking forward to our next wedding anniversary now! However, the future belongs to our Heavenly Father…*
>
> *During the past two months we have been busy catching up with*

various tasks, in particular semi-permanent fences of fibre-glass
rods and two electrified high-tensile steel wires, on both sides of the
drains that are like small canals, as in the past someone had made
them too wide… also it is best to stop the stock drinking from
them, as they tend to damage the sides and make them even wider.
Gideon has also made some fresh crossings of the drains that make
stock moving much easier at flood time. We also plan to make three
cattle races during the next few weeks using poly rods and wire. The
electric fence improvements should cut our routine electric fence
moving by about 60 per cent or more, next we plan to subdivide
more of the paddocks with poly rods…

Our sheep mainly live on the hills, we also enjoy mustering
them, watching them follow the leaders, we do not use dogs, just
quietly follow them, they seem to be becoming much more friendly.
We hope they will eventually learn to come when called, by
recognizing our voices, as they did in Biblical times…

And so the life of the farm goes on, day after day after day, all
described in the minutest detail. But that doesn't mean they have
no time for fun and socializing.

Recently we went to an excellent presentation about sharing the
good news of the Saviour in Arab countries by folk who had lived
and worked in North Africa and the Middle East for many years.
While fundamental Islam is lethal, it was thought that overall only
2 per cent of the total Arab population actually had a heart belief

in Islam. The other 98 per cent believed in something else, or at
least were only nominally Muslim.

And so the life of the farm goes on, and on. Now and again they
are able to look at the wider picture:

> Most New Zealanders are appalled at the moral landslide affecting
> the country, though trends are comparable to most of the rest of the
> Western world. New Zealand, like the rest, has suffered from
> decades of humanistic socialism, liberal education and the so-called
> women's lib. The promotion of evolution as a fact rather than as a
> theory – in the media as well as places of learning, has done much
> to undermine Godly values and attitudes. The West is now reaping
> its fruit.

They finish with a few thoughts on the role of the European Union
and how, in league with the British government, it is destroying
British farming – which might well be true. Indeed, a sign comes
from an unlikely source:

> Walking on the hills, we surprised a lone sheep who had lost sight
> of her flock. So startled did she look that I asked her, 'what's the
> matter, then?' She eyed me for a moment or two, then uttered a very
> distinct 'blair' before bolting off. She left me wondering if she had
> deep political insight.

Then, after nine closely typed A4 pages, they finish with a personal note to their addressees:

We hope you have a lovely holiday together. Gideon has prepared some photos to go with this.

Really? Has he? Do tell him to take his time, there's absolutely no rush…

The Vice of Vituperation

I PERSONALLY don't hate round robin letters, even the ones we receive at home – though not many of them arrive these days. They can be annoying, though more often unintentionally hilarious. After all, you don't have to read every one of those computer specifications, the list of the children's GCSEs, or the minute-by-minute account of the holiday in Peru. And there is a certain *schadenfreude* to be extracted from the things that have gone terribly wrong. Some of these are merely hinted at: 'Emily brings joy and laughter to our lives', if unaccompanied by a list of academic qualifications and musical accomplishments, can indicate learning difficulties.

But other recipients of the letters are less tolerant. For me, among the delights of being sent so many hundreds of letters every year are the covering notes, some of them almost literally smothered in rage and bile. For example, one dated from Christmas 2004 has five chunks torn out of it. The reader has written over the top: 'our dog felt the same way about this letter, and tried to eat it'. Small wonder, since it includes some particularly infuriating paragraphs, such as this about the senders' twenty-one-year-old son:

HE HAS *been taken on by a US conglomerate based in Slough. He is being paid a fantastic salary and has his own desk, telephone, parking space et al. His title is marketing assistant, and involves travelling all over the UK to give presentations to oil and electricity generating bigwigs. When his line manager is abroad, he is allowed to drive the company car (Jaguar or Saab).*

Here's another typical example of recipient rage:

I ENCLOSE *a round robin letter which would not fail to bore you stupid. I left their home town over ten years ago and hardly knew the children mentioned, so I found the whole letter smug, boring, and of no interest whatsoever. Sorry if I sound unkind.*

No, please don't apologize!

AT LEAST *the Parkers can be relied on for consistency — they are all still gifted, multi-talented, and smug!*

The Parkers' letter caused extra fury, since near the end it reveals that the sender's husband is about to sack almost all the workforce in his company. A typically jaunty paragraph reads:

ANDY *and his brother have concluded that the business is unsustainable, and are now in the process of all but closing it, reducing to about 10 per cent. It's a blow they cannot help but take on a personal level. Their dad founded the company in 1947, average length of service is twenty years, some employees have never worked anywhere else, and many are each other's fathers, brothers, nephews and in-laws. Let's hope this difficult decision will prove a move for the better for everyone.*

As the recipient writes in her covering letter:

THE FACT *that he is sacking 90 per cent of his workforce rates just this one short paragraph. I just hope none of the employees are on her mailing list.*

If they were, they would receive along with their P45s jolly news of the family's skiing trips to the Alps and their luxurious holiday in Sorrento.

Other letters create feelings of nausea which are just as strong for different reasons.

PLEASE *find enclosed a truly horrific round robin, which you can use in your new book Christmas With The Fokkers. I shared a flat with Jenny in the early 70s, and I can only think that she has either had a frontal lobotomy or has embraced Stepford principles wholeheartedly.*

THIS *letter was sent by a person with whom I had a brief fling thirty years ago. It ended entirely without acrimony, but it did end with total finality, and we have had no communication with each other since — apart, that is, from the Christmas newsletter, which started turning up about eight years ago. The thing is that there are fourteen or fifteen people mentioned in the letter — at least I assume they are all people. I suppose 'Edith' could be a faithful old sheepdog – and I have not the remotest idea who any of them are.*

I AM *enclosing this year's offering from Vanessa, which I always find cloying and yucky. Unfortunately, the letter does not show how very, very clever Vanessa must be, as she's been writing to us every year since she was a foetus.*

Some people are more inclined to resent the time and effort implied by being sent these letters. Why, they ask, should I use energy I could be devoting to watching *Celebrity Love Island* or watching paint dry?

THESE *people's letters always induce a great depression in me. I particularly liked the part about the garden, with the two indistinguishable 'before' and 'after' pictures.*

Indeed the pictures are almost identical, with one barely noticeable difference:

BEFORE *the summer we did a bit of work in the garden. At the end of the lawn at the back we have a number of Leylandii. Nothing much grows under them, so we decided to replace the weeds with decorative stones and plants in pots. We also got a composter. It is to the left of the view above. It took only a few weeks to fill it up, and we have not yet taken any compost out of it. The amount of grass cuttings produced would fill a dozen composters, so we still have to make trips to the refuse tip with the excess.*

Or here is the account of their summer holiday. It is clear that the family as a whole is close to losing the will to live; what maddens the readers is the sense that they wish to transfer their malaise to everyone else:

> *This summer we spent twelve nights camping in France. This was at the back end of August, when it rained just about every day. The intention was to have an easy, beach-based holiday as the camp site was only a short walk from the beach. We did manage a couple of days in the sun. We sailed from Portsmouth to Cherbourg and drove down to Dinard, which is near St Malo. As we could not spend much time on the beach we drove to various towns in the area. We went to Fougères, Saint Suliac, Dinan and Mt. St. Michel. The girls could practise their French buying bread and croissants every morning on the site. Isobel has since started doing French at school and is getting on well…*

Please, no more! It is unsurprising that some recipients seem driven to the edge of their reason by these letters. It's hard to know what is more aggravating – boastfulness or boringness. Take this letter from Canada which brought much grief to the English people who received it:

> *How are things with us? Well, as Canadians, we tend to be upbeat about everything! So the answer is 'Good!' A while ago, I asked a friend who is more dour than most, 'How's it going?' He replied, 'good and bad'. That is probably about as honest and complete an*

answer as anyone can give. And we're all likely the same. But for those of you who are interested, here is a rundown of what we have done in the last year. There has been so much to be thankful for, and yet some things that we wish could have been better.

By this time, the average recipient is in a deep and peaceful trance. But other letters create the opposite effect, sending fiery currents of rage coursing through the readers' veins.

I CAN hardly begin to tell you about my feelings for these appalling people. Please put them in your next book and name them! Why should they get away with it? I only know them because I was at school with her. She was head girl, and had a huge bosom. I haven't seen her in twenty years, thank God, but I bet the bust is of double-decker proportions now.

Rich, smug and revolting, 42-foot yachts, perfect house, bloody great mediaeval barns — can it get any worse? I want to kill them. Mind you, I think that every time their hideous newsletter arrives, and then next year's offering comes along, and it is always worse. I suppose we'll have the details of the sodding wedding next time round... Oh God, I can't go on. Even writing about them makes me ill.

The powerful desire to mete out death to letter-writers is a frequent theme:

IT'S the all-round smugness that gets me. They are both senior lecturers and nice people – till now! This made me want to go round and throttle them.

Some people find news from the former colonies particularly grating:

THIS *classic example is hot off my aunt's printer in Adelaide. It is, yet again, more badly constructed and punctuated drivel. As if having to read such sublime comments as 'it was very biblical in places like Damascus and Mount Sinai' wasn't enough, she goes on to write about our lives in the UK!*

Which she does, complacently describing how her mother-in-law has been helped by the installation of a new stairlift – and sending this information to the very people who arranged for it to be installed, without giving them credit for their work.

But telling people news about themselves can be a hazard in letters sent to dozens, perhaps hundreds. One reader writes from a rectory in Lancashire:

I WAS *reminded of a newsletter I received some years ago while working abroad. It was from a well-meaning but busybody family I knew slightly, and ran to several sides of A4. I was faintly surprised even to receive the letter, and very surprised to read an entire paragraph in it about me, along the lines of 'our minister's wife is…' with full details of what I was doing, why and where, written by people I barely knew for people I had never met. That felt weird.*

Almost as weird as the chap in Somerset must have felt when he got a lengthy newsletter, with the death of his own wife tucked away in half a paragraph, crammed in amid the news of exotic holidays and the addition of a new sun lounge:

> ... ALSO *the death of our dear friend Carol, who put up a brave struggle against lymphoma. Our thoughts are with Nigel and his sons this Christmas...*

... they wrote to Nigel.

A new menace is the website Friends Reunited. It was through them that a couple in Essex began to receive round robins from another couple who had been fellow pupils in the wife's primary school class fifty-five years ago. She had not met them during the course of the following five and a half decades.

> THIS *letter is typical, exhorting us to think more about other people than ourselves, to be grateful for our many blessings, and usually ending with a little homily leaving us in no doubt about what selfish people we are. I can just about stomach the fact that they enjoy a direct line to the Lord, but the overall sanctimonious tone makes me feel quite unwell.*

And you can see her point:

> IN JUNE *we had our second Scarecrow Festival, with our tiny hamlet producing another sixty different scarecrows. It was highly successful and the Good Lord looked very kindly on us with a*

weekend of sunshine, and it was dry underfoot from the previous week. Austin has kept records of our weather down here for the last ten years, and they make interesting reading. We have had more rain this year. Unfortunately we do not have the means of measuring the sunshine... this year we have decided to donate to charity instead of giving gifts. It seems that all of us who have so much should share it with those who have nothing.

Thank you for that thought, which of course had never occurred to any of us.

As the chapter on religion shows, many people imagine that the Almighty personally arranges the weather for their convenience and delight.

BACK *in July Dad was eighty, so we had a celebration meal. Church friends joined him and Mum, as well as other close friends. It was a good day, and the Lord blessed us with lovely weather and we were able to enjoy the beautiful grounds, with the wildlife and the lake. We were left very well fed, and not wanting to eat the following day.*

An effect not uncommon among the readers of such letters. As the recipient of that one wrote:

THE LAST *time I saw this person was eight years ago, and she subsequently accused me — without explaining to me what I was supposed to have done — of having spoiled her parents' fiftieth anniversary party. Do you suppose that perhaps the continued*

despatch of these letters might be seen as a form of prolonged
punishment?

It is curious how a complete lack of response rarely makes a difference to the senders of round robins.

THIS *arrives every year addressed to my parents, who are both*
dead. It is from the daughter of a very distant (and also dead)
friend of my mother's, and she hated receiving the letter every year.
The senders do not provide their address, so I cannot return it
unopened and so stop this annual torment!

Occasionally the letters are not so terrible – at least not as bad as
some others. That does not stop their unlucky readers from
foaming at the mouth, biting the arms of sofas, barking at the dog,
and so forth.

I THINK *you might agree that the whole tone of this letter is self-*
serving, and designed to create an impression of general all-round-
aren't-we-super-people-ness. There are two paragraphs that really
do it for me, though. One is the totally pointless reference to staying
in 'Landmark Trust property number 20', and the other has to be
the unbelievable '. . . we spotted some more stars at Jani's [who the
hell is Jani?] opening night. . . but more importantly saw her to be
a star'. The final joy of that phrase is the comment in brackets:
'(Dave is now engaged to Selma)', like a conspiratorial aside to the
knowing. And I don't know any of them!

> *So, apart from discovering that they had chicken pox, stayed in a lot of posh properties, and hob-nobbed with famous people such as Rick Stein, I have learned that the wife is doing terribly well with her choreography, does selfless work for the community and combines raising 'two gorgeous chaps' with full-time work at The Elms. What a woman. How nice of her to let me know…*

Oh dear, I feel that the sender should be more careful next year, and get someone else to pre-read the letter, otherwise cardiac arrest might result.

Some people also relish the bad news.

> I DON'T *know how many Christmas letters you get with pictures of legs with bolts through them, but here is one. The mother's delight at the violence of injury to her daughter can be attributed to her nursing training…*

And the details are in the letter:

> MARTHA *was off to Pony Club for a week, and this is where the drama started! On the second day she was involved in a very bad accident when the horse fell back on her and broke her leg (the right femur was snapped clean in two.) She was blue-lighted to hospital by ambulance, and underwent minor surgery to stick a bolt through the bottom of her shin so she could go on traction (see right)…*

And there it is, for the delectation of all her parents' acquaintance:

a young girl's leg with a Frankenstein's monster-style bolt through it.

However, it's intriguing how newsletter writers are often slow to show concern about other people's mishaps.

> I ENCLOSE *a round robin letter from Somerset… this former friend has never once responded to my hand-written card telling her that my husband had had a heart attack. I have merely had this rubbish in reply. She is now struck off our Christmas card list, as these letters make me so angry.*

The rage sometimes just bubbles over:

> THIS *letter, by my brother-in-law, is simply designed to make the rest of us know how tawdry and uninteresting our lives are compared to the Campbells.*

The accompanying missive, from Scotland, certainly starts in challenging fashion:

> 2004 *has been memorable in the Campbell nest for Poughkeepsie's mastery of disembowelling mice in total darkness.* [Poughkeepsie is a cat, named after the town in New York state]… *Nightly, at almost exactly 2 a.m., for the past six months, Angus and Morag have been woken by the gently rhythmic cracking of bones just inches from their unseeing eyes. At dawn, the first rays of sun glint across the neatly dissected silhouette of the rejected stomach on the pillow…*

Thankfully, the rest of the four-page letter reverts to the usual parade of academic and sporting success, interrupted only by costly and exotic holidays.

A reader from north London sends in two newsletters:

CLIVE *and Debs lived two doors away from me for four years. Their house was originally owned by her grandmother, who lived there for many years and whom my mother and I knew on a polite, neighbourly 'hello' basis. I had absolutely nothing in common with them and found another polite 'hello' often best avoided, as any ensuing conversation would always entail lengthy, self-centred monologues from them.*

Phyllis was Debs's mother, who died two years ago, and Roy, her father, still lives in their house in the next road. I do not know him, except by sight. He would not know me — thankfully! — and neither would the dog, if you can call that a dog.

The picture implies that it is indeed a rather small and yappy-looking canine. However, nothing prevents Roy from sending his newsletter to a woman whom he would not even recognize if he met her in the street. Like many older people, he does seem to lead a life of necessarily limited excitment:

RECENTLY, *my faithful TV in its nice wooden cabinet (remember when all televisions were housed in wood? This one was over twenty years old) decided it had had enough and died on me. I thought that as I did not watch TV that often I would wait until the sales before replacing it, but strangely I missed them. So I splashed out on a nice new, up to date piece of equipment. I must say that TV sets have improved over the last twenty-plus years. I might enjoy watching TV and the occasional video, but not too much.*

But enjoying his new TV, though not too much, isn't all he does.

Musically, I continue with my accordion, including lessons. I also continue with visits to Glyndebourne...

Without, one hopes, the accordion, which would not be welcomed during an adventurous new production of *The Magic Flute*.

Back to Clive and Debs who, it turns out, were great fans of Concorde:

CONCORDE has not disappeared from our lives, even though she is no longer flying. We have already visited the Manchester exhibit — Daisy finally got to see the inside of Concorde! There were many auctions held after her retirement [Concorde's not Daisy's] to sell off all the spares and memorabilia. We now have some bizarre items around the house and garden, including an exhaust gas temperature thermo-couple, three cockpit dials, an explosion detector, engine and reheat components, landing gear wheel rims — the list goes on. Some stuff we have purchased for resale, such as Concorde Sennheiser headphones, pens, cutlery, glasses and Wedgwood stuff.

However, the pinnacle of our collection has to be the TOILET

CUBICLE!!! Which won us a piece in The Scotsman *newspaper, as well as a big article in the* Daily Express *— for some reason, the press find the idea of a Concorde toilet sitting in our lounge strangely and hilariously worthy of coverage…*

Hard to understand.

Another letter is the usual gallimaufry of examination successes, and superb holidays – in Peru (why do so many round robin writers wind up in Machu Picchu? Is it a sort of secret convention centre where they can share notes about how to infuriate their readers?) – plus trips to Portugal, Italy and Wales. Only one bad thing happens to any of them:

JANET *had a year of toothache, that ended with an hour and a half in the dentist's chair, and three nerves removed!*

As the recipient remarks:

OUR *feelings of indifference towards these people, who are our neighbours, have now been transformed into loathing, and a profound sorrow that the toothache has been cured.*

Some readers, by contrast, are consumed more by sorrow than by anger:

THIS *is from some very old friends, but I cannot help but feel slightly embarrassed for them, rather like overhearing a very elderly relative break wind at Christmas dinner.*

The letter referred to does include some rather sweet, even plangent lines:

> FEWER *guests have visited this year, for no apparent reason.*

This next letter accompanied a round robin from landowners, who devoted it mainly to – no doubt well-justified – complaints about the DEFRA bureaucracy.

> THE REFORM *of the Common Agricultural Policy and the finalization of the Scottish Outdoor Access Code reared their ugly heads and required much study . . .*

The recipients write:

> THIS *letter was sent to us by a couple who we met twenty-five years ago and have not seen since. We receive the same ghastly letter every Christmas, relating their tales of woe and cattle or land purchases, interspersed with stories of their many holidays. They live in a castle in Scotland – see photo by their talented daughter.*
>
> *It all got too much for one of my own daughters three years ago, so she returned their letter to them with the words, 'I believe you have mistaken me for someone who gives a fuck.' She sent it unsigned. In the past two years, my daughters have annotated the letters and returned the first from Belfast, and the other from Madrid.*

Which is one way of getting your revenge.

Others include writing furious annotations in the margins of the letters. For example, this letter tackles the writer's daughter and son-in-law:

> TERRY *is very clever, he has two degrees, also he just passed his Masters and his graduation is in two weeks. Elinor is different, down to earth, basically not academic, doesn't care about that, but has more sense than Terry. If you want anything organized, ask Elinor. If you want a nail knocking in, ask Elinor. In fact, if you want anything, ask Elinor, Terry is hopeless. It works, though, we take him as he is, we've known him long enough now.*

As the recipient writes, 'what is her poor son-in-law supposed to make of this?'

Another form of revenge is to send spoof letters in return. The theory is that these will subtly expose to the original senders how ridiculous the concept can be.

> EMILY *is back working in Manchester. She has a new pimp, which is a great relief to us, since the last one was violent and insisted on sending her to some quite unsuitable clients. Jonty's crack cocaine business goes from strength to strength...*

The problem is that some people don't realize it's a spoof, and even those who do often don't get the joke, since they don't see anything strange about the letters they send in the first place. Because if they did, why would they send them? And what would their readers have to do to get their New Year off with a rousing, stimulating, cathartic, pipe-clearing shout of sheer rage?